Listen In

BOOK
1

Second Edition

David Nunan

THOMSON

HEINLE

Australia · Canada · Mexico · Singapore · Spain · United Kingdom · United States

THOMSON
★ ™
HEINLE

Listen In, Second Edition, **Student Book 1**
David Nunan

Publisher, Global ELT: Christopher Wenger
Editorial Manager: Sean Bermingham
Development Editor: Ross Wallace
Production Editor: Tan Jin Hock
ELT Directors: John Lowe (Asia),
   Francisco Lozano (Latin America)

Director of Marketing, ESL/ELT: Amy Mabley
Marketing Manager: Ian Martin
Interior/Cover Design: Christopher Hanzie, TYA Inc.
Illustrations: Raketshop Design Studio, Philippines
Composition: Stella Tan, TYA Inc.
Printer: Seng Lee Press

Printed in Singapore
1 2 3 4 5 6 7 8 9 10   06 05 04 03 02

For permission to use material from this text or product, contact us in the United States:
Tel   1-800-730-2214
Fax   1-800-730-2215
Web www.thomsonrights.com

For more information, contact Heinle, 25 Thomson Place, Boston, Massachusetts 02210 USA, or you can visit our Internet site at http://www.heinle.com

ISBN 0-8384-0408-1

Photo Credits

Unless otherwise stated, all photos are from PhotoDisc, Inc. Digital Imagery © copyright 2002 PhotoDisc, Inc.

Photos on the cover, title page, pages 7, 11 (top), 13, 15 (top), 19 (top), 23 (top), 25 (woman with headphones), 26, 27 (top), 31 (top), 37 (top), 41 (top), 45 (top), 49 (top), 53 (top: left and third from left), 59 (top), 62 (bottom two rows), 63 (top), 67 (top), 68 (center), 71 (top), 75 (top), 81 (top), 85 (top), 89 (top), 93 (top), and 97 (top) are the exclusive property of Heinle.

Photos from other sources:

Page 24 (left): © Associated Press

Page 24 (center): © Derick A. Thomas: Dat's Jazz/ CORBIS

Page 24 (right): © Reuters NewMedia Inc./CORBIS

Pages 46–48, page 69 (bottom right): © Hong Kong Tourism Board

Page 69 (bottom left): TYA Inc.

Page 84: © Associated Press

Every effort has been made to trace all sources of illustrations/ photos/information in this book, but if any have been inadvertently overlooked, the publisher will be pleased to make the necessary arrangements at the first opportunity.

Author's Acknowledgments

First and foremost, I would like to thank Chris Wenger, whose vision for this project matched mine, and who readily understood what I was trying to achieve. Sean Bermingham and Ross Wallace have made a great editorial team, and really took the pain out of the revision process. Heartfelt thanks are also due to the friends, colleagues, and acquaintances who helped in the collection of the authentic data on which the materials are based—you all helped in the creation of a truly special series. Thanks to Dennis Hogan and Tan Tat Chu for their support in paving the way for the second edition, and also to Bob Cullen who astonishes me with his ability to monitor the many projects and initiatives that Thomson Learning has under development.

In addition to the above, I extend my appreciation to the following people, all of whom have helped to make this series a pleasure to work on: Amy Mabley, John Lowe, Ian Martin, Francisco Lozano, and Tan Jin Hock at Thomson Learning; Christopher Hanzie, Stella Tan, and the staff at T.Y.A.; Leo Cultura and the staff at Raketshop Design Studio.

I am also very grateful to the following professionals who provided invaluable comments and suggestions during the development of this series:

Brett Bowie	Konkuk University, Korea
Marlene Brenes	Benemerita University, Mexico
Grace Chang	Tak Ming College, Taiwan
Grace Chao	Soochow University, Taiwan
Jim Chou	National Chengchi University, Taiwan
Susana Christie	San Diego State University, USA
Karen Cisney	Soochow University, Taiwan
Carla Diez	ITESM, Mexico
Michael Fox	Seoul National University of Education, Korea
Chiu-hua Fu	Van Nung Institute of Technology, Taiwan
Pierre Gauvin	Sung Dong ECC, Korea
Frank Graziani	Tokai University, Japan
Ann-Marie Hadzima	National Taiwan University, Taiwan
Patti Hedden	Yonsei University, Korea
Angela Hou	Fu-Jen Catholic University, Taiwan
Yu-chen Hso	Soochow University, Taiwan
Ju-ying Vinia Huang	Tamkang University, Taiwan
Yuko Iwata	Tokai University, Japan
Inga Jelescheff	Saguragaoka High School, Japan
Monica Kamio	AEON Amity, Japan
Alexis Kim	English City Institute, Korea
Mia Kim	Kyunghee University, Korea
Jane King	Soochow University, Taiwan
Mary Ying-hsiu Ku	Taipei Municipal First Girl's High School, Taiwan
Balk-eum Lee	Aju University Education Center, Korea
Cheri Lee	One World Language Institute, Korea
Jenny Lee	Seoul National University of Education, Korea
Li-te Li	Tung Fang B & E Vocational High School, Taiwan
Jui-hsiang Lu	Van Nung Institute of Technology, Taiwan
Shiona MacKenzie	Gakashuin Boys' Senior High School, Japan
Rhona McCrae	Freelance English Instructor, Japan
Michael Noonan	Kookmin University, Korea
Maria Ordoñez	Universidad de Celaya, Mexico
Daisy Pan	Van Nung Institute of Technology, Taiwan
Jason Park	Korea University of Foreign Studies, Korea
Young Park	Dankook University, Korea
Kerry Read	Blossom English Center, Japan
Lesley Riley	Kanazawa Institute of Technology, Japan
Cathy Rudnick	Hanyang University, Korea
Kathy Sherak	San Francisco State University, USA
Yoshiko Shimizu	Osaka College of Foreign Languages, Japan
John Smith	International Osaka Owada Koko, Japan
Sue Sohn	Sung Dong ECC, Korea
May Tang	National Taiwan University, Taiwan
Yu-hsin Tsai	Chinese Culture University, Taiwan
Melanie Vandenhoeven	Sungshin University, Korea
Holly Winber	Senzoku Gakuen Fuzoku Koko, Japan
Jane Wu	Fu-Jen Catholic University, Taiwan
Hsiao-tsui Yang	Shih Chien University, Taiwan
Hai-young Yun	Korea Development Institute, Korea

Scope and Sequence

Unit	Title/Topic	Goals	Sources	Pronunciation
Starter *Page 8*	*Learning to listen.* **Listening skills**	Identifying different types of listening	Casual conversations Telephone conversations Sports broadcast	Intonation to show surprise
1 *Page 12*	*Pleased to meet you.* **Introductions**	Understanding greetings and introductions Confirming people's names	Telephone conversation Party conversations	Number of syllables in words
2 *Page 16*	*This is my family.* **Family**	Identifying family members	Casual conversations	Contrast of /s/ and /z/
3 *Page 20*	*He's the one in the blue shirt.* **Appearance**	Identifying people through physical description	Office conversation Party conversations	Contrast of question and statement intonation
4 *Page 24*	*Do you like rock?* **Music**	Identifying likes and dislikes Identifying different genres of music	Casual conversations Radio broadcast	Word stress
5 *Page 28*	*It's a really interesting place.* **Cities**	Understanding descriptions of places Identifying where people are from	Conversations at a convention	Contrast of /z/ and /zh/
1–5 *Page 32*	**Review**		Casual conversations Radio broadcast	
6 *Page 34*	*This is where I live.* **Homes**	Understanding descriptions of homes	Casual conversation Telephone inquiry	Voiced/unvoiced *th*
7 *Page 38*	*Where is the furniture department?* **Shopping**	Identifying locations in a store Recognizing ordinal numbers in rapid speech	Face-to-face inquiries Store announcement	Ordinal numbers
8 *Page 42*	*Can you work weekends?* **Jobs**	Identifying abilities Identifying preferences	Casual conversations Job interviews	Word stress
9 *Page 46*	*Where's the ferry terminal?* **Sightseeing**	Identifying locations in a city Understanding directions	Conversations with hotel concierge Tour narration	Contrast of *yes/no* and *wh-* question intonation
10 *Page 50*	*How does it work?* **Technology**	Understanding instructions Following sequence of events	Casual conversations Telephone inquiry Conversation with sales clerk	Contrast of intonation for certainty and uncertainty
6–10 *Page 54*	**Review**		Telephone inquiry Job interview Telephone recording Face-to-face inquiries	

Unit	Title/Topic	Goals	Sources	Pronunciation
11 *Page 56*	*I usually get up at six.* **Routines**	Identifying times and events Understanding schedules	Conversation with school counselor	Reduced form of *do you*
12 *Page 60*	*I'll have soup and a sandwich.* **Food**	Understanding food and drink orders Understanding and confirming reservations	Telephone inquiries Conversation with restaurant server	Reduced forms of *would, will*
13 *Page 64*	*He shoots, he scores!* **Sports**	Identifying sports Understanding sports broadcasts	Sports commentaries Radio sports report	Intonation for *Oh*
14 *Page 68*	*Do you want to see a movie?* **Entertainment**	Recognizing invitations Identifying types of entertainment	Telephone recording Casual conversations	Question intonation
15 *Page 72*	*What's the weather like?* **Weather**	Identifying types of weather Understanding weather reports	News and weather reports Casual conversations	Word stress
11–15 *Page 76*	**Review**		Casual conversations Sports interview Sports broadcast	
16 *Page 78*	*How did you meet your wife?* **Meeting people**	Identifying people through description Understanding a personal narrative	Casual conversations Dating service recordings	Reduced forms of *kind of, sort of*
17 *Page 82*	*Why don't we buy a new car?* **Suggestions**	Recognizing suggestions Understanding objections	Telephone conversations Casual conversations	Omitted words
18 *Page 86*	*She's kind of shy.* **Personality**	Identifying personal qualities Understanding survey questions	Casual conversations Survey interview	Phonemic distinctions
19 *Page 90*	*Are you free on Tuesday?* **Appointments**	Understanding schedules Identifying and confirming appointments	Casual conversations Telephone conversations	Contrast of /ay/ and /e/
20 *Page 94*	*How do you like to learn?* **Learning styles**	Identifying learning styles Understanding information in a lecture	Short lecture Oral test	Syllable stress and sentence rhythm
16–20 *Page 98*	**Review**		Dating service recordings Casual conversations	

To the Student

Dear Student,

Welcome to *Listen In*. This three-level series will give you many opportunities to develop your listening skills. It will also help you improve your speaking skills. There are several important features of the series that may be unfamiliar to you. They include real-life tasks, real-life language, and learning strategies.

Real-life tasks

The tasks you do in *Listen In* are all based on the kinds of listening that you do in real life, such as following directions, listening to telephone messages, and understanding the news and weather.

Real-life language

The listening materials are also taken from real life. You will hear many different kinds of recorded language, including conversations, telephone messages, store announcements, news and weather broadcasts, and public announcements.

Learning strategies

In addition to teaching you language, *Listen In* also focuses on learning strategies. In completing the tasks, you will use strategies that will improve your listening inside and outside the classroom.

Each level of *Listen In* consists of a Starter Unit to get you thinking about the listening strategies in the book, as well as giving you some practice using those strategies. There are 20 main units and four Review units. Linked to each of the main units is a page of Self Study Practice at the back of the book. Here is what each unit contains:

Warm up Task

This section is designed to introduce you to the topic for the unit and present some of the important vocabulary and expressions that you will hear and eventually use in the unit.

Listening Tasks

You will then hear a number of different listening passages, all of which relate to the target language of that unit. One of the listening tasks in each unit focuses on pronunciation; another type of task allows you to decide on your own response. The *Listen for it* boxes highlight useful words and expressions commonly used in everyday speech. The teacher will ask you to listen to most passages more than once. This will give you the chance to understand more of what you hear, use a variety of listening strategies, and check your answers to the listening tasks.

Your Turn!

The last page gives you the opportunity to practice the target language you have been listening to. *Try this . . .* is a communicative task that you complete in pairs or in groups. The *Sample Dialog* and *Useful Expressions* will help you to complete this task. *In Focus* gives you cultural information that you can discuss as a class.

Self Study Practice

After class, you can get extra listening practice by turning to the back of the book (pages 107–127) and completing the Self Study Practice Units.

The main thing to remember when you are using these materials is to relax and enjoy yourself as you learn. In some units, you will hear conversations in which you will not understand every word. This does not matter. Not even native English speakers understand or listen for every single word. This series will help you develop strategies for understanding the most important information.

I had a great time creating *Listen In*. I hope that you enjoy using these materials as much as I enjoyed writing them.

Good luck!

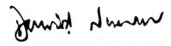

Classroom Language

Could you repeat that, please?

Could you play it again, please?

Could you turn up the volume, please?

How do you say . . . in English?

What does . . . mean?

How do you spell . . . ?

I'm not sure.

Sorry, I don't understand.

What did you get for question number one?

What's your answer for number two?

Starter UNIT

Learning to listen.

Goals
- Identifying different types of listening
- Identifying different types of listening tasks

1 *Before listening, it's useful to think about the topic and focus on the key words and expressions that you are likely to hear.*

A **Each of the people has difficulty listening in English. Check (✔) the boxes next to the problems you share.**

Most people talk so fast that I can't understand much of what they say.

I can usually understand some of the words but I don't always get the main point.

I can't always pick out the most important words when someone is talking to me.

I can't understand a lot of the slang expressions I hear.

My vocabulary just isn't big enough to understand everything that someone says to me.

Sometimes I get confused between two words that sound similar but have different meanings.

B **These words appear frequently in the *Listen In* series. Do you know what they mean? If not, check with a partner or look them up in a dictionary.**

compare	pronunciation	repeat	intonation	identify
expression	brainstorm	role play	syllable	recognize

C **Brainstorm! Work with a partner. List two or three other problems you have with listening in English.**

We listen for many reasons. For example, we sometimes listen to get the gist of what we are hearing. That means we try to understand in general what is being talked about.

A **Listen and number the pictures (1–4).**

The people are talking about a (hotel / restaurant).

The man is talking about (sports / weather).

1

The people are talking about a (movie / concert).

The people are talking about a (school / company).

B **Listen again. What are the people talking about? Circle the correct answer for each.**

Sometimes we listen to get the main idea of what is being said. Sometimes we listen for key details.

A **Listen to the conversations and check (✔) the main idea for each one.**

1. __✔__ Carol is looking for a new job.   ____ Carol likes her new job.

2. ____ Adam doesn't want to get married.   ____ Adam is getting married.

3. ____ Keiko bought a car.   ____ Keiko sold her car.

4. ____ Jim can't go to the party.   ____ Jim doesn't like parties.

5. ____ Andrea can't find her wallet.   ____ Andrea found a lost wallet.

B **Listen again and fill in the correct details.**

1. Carol studied _____ at university.

2. Adam is _____ years old.

3. Keiko is using her _____ car.

4. Jim finishes work at _____ o'clock tomorrow night.

5. Andrea's _____ arrives in five minutes.

Learning to listen.

In real life, people don't just listen, they listen and do something, such as deciding what to wear after hearing a weather report. In this task, you are listening to three people and making a decision based on what you hear.

A Three people are talking about the methods they use to improve their listening skills. Listen and fill in the blanks.

Gloria

I listen to a lot of *English songs* _____.
I also spend time _____.

Francisco

One of the things I do is listen to _____.
Another is to just walk up to _____ and start a conversation.

Min-hee

I've got all kinds of _____ that I use to practice. Oh, and I also listen to the _____ on the radio.

B Listen again and check your answers. Which methods are *you* going to use to improve your listening skills? Write them below, then share with a partner.

_____

*Listening sometimes means focusing not just on **what** people say but the **way** they say it. This means paying attention to pronounciation, stress, sentence rhythm, and intonation. In this task, you are listening for the speaker's intonation.*

A Listen to the examples. In which one is the speaker surprised? Circle the correct answer.

• Example 1   • Example 2

Listen and decide if the people are stating a fact or expressing surprise. Circle *F* for *fact* or *S* for *surprise*.

1. F S   2.   F S   3.   F S   4.   F S   5.   F S   6.   F S

B Listen again and practice.

In real life, people typically respond to what they hear. In this task, you are listening to questions and deciding on your own response.

Listen and circle the answers that are right for you.

1. Yes, I do.   I don't mind it.   No, not really.

2. listening   speaking   writing   reading

3. They talk too fast.   They use a lot of slang.   I can't understand all the words.

Your Turn!

Talking about ways of practising listening

Sample Dialog

A: Do you ever listen to music in English?
B: Yes, I like to listen to American rock music.
A: What's your favorite group?
B: I really like a band called Radiohead. How about you?
A: I don't really listen to much music. I prefer movies.
B: What's your favorite movie in English?
A: My favorite movies are 'Titanic' and 'Gladiator.'

Useful Expressions

- How many hours do you spend studying outside of class?
- I try to practice listening for about an hour every night.
- How much do you understand when you listen in English?
- I guess about fifty or sixty percent.
- Which is harder for you, listening or speaking?
- They're both hard but I think listening is a little harder.

Try this . . . Ask other students the questions. When someone says 'Yes,' write down the person's name. Ask follow-up questions to find out more information.

Do you . . .	Name	More Information
listen to music in English?	_____	_____
watch English-language movies?	_____	_____
listen to English-language books on tape?	_____	_____
take listening tests in English?	_____	_____
have conversations with English speakers?	_____	_____

In Focus: *Why study English?*

English is widely known as the language of international trade but doing business isn't the only reason to learn the language. There are probably almost as many reasons to study English as there are people who want to learn it. Some people study English to help them get a good job. Others are preparing to travel to English-speaking countries. *What's the main reason that you're studying English?*

I'm studying to pass my entrance exam for college.

I work at a hotel so I have to speak English to our guests.

I just want to understand more of the dialog in Hollywood movies.

Learning to listen.

Pleased to meet you.

Goals • Understanding greetings and introductions
• Confirming people's names

1

A **What do people say when they meet for the first time? Check (✔) the boxes.**

☐ How do you do?
☐ What are you doing?
☐ Hi, how's it going?
☐ Pleased to meet you.

☐ I'm going now.
☐ Hello. I'm John.
☐ Nice to meet you.
☐ What's the matter?

☐ Hi, my name's Amy.
☐ Good to see you again.
☐ Good morning.
☐ I don't think we've met . . .

What might the people in each picture be saying?

B **Brainstorm!** In informal situations, people often use an 'icebreaker' before introducing themselves. Work with a partner. Make a list of icebreakers you could use when meeting someone at a party.

Hi. Are you a friend of John's?

Are you enjoying the party?

Hey, have you tried the sushi?

2

A Listen. How many voices do you hear? Circle a number.

1   2   3   4   5   6

B Listen again and check (✔) the names you hear.

- ☐ Tia
- ☐ Mila
- ☐ Erika
- ☐ Leanne
- ☐ Enrique
- ☐ Li-wen
- ☐ John
- ☐ Joan
- ☐ Tina
- ☐ Mia

3

A Listen and check (✔) the names that have two syllables.

- ☐ Alison
- ☐ Karen
- ☐ Jeena
- ☐ Sarah
- ☐ David
- ☐ Paul
- ☐ Yumiko
- ☐ Sulinko
- ☐ Tony
- ☐ Alan

B Listen again and practice.

4

A Listen to the conversation between Leanne and John. Write the names of the people they decide to invite to their party.

Listen for it

No problem is an informal way of saying you're willing to do something.

Guest List

John and Tina Lowe

B Listen again and check your answers.

5

A Read the names below. Then look at the picture and listen to the conversations. Number the people in the picture (1–6).

1. Yumiko Sato
2. Tina Lowe
3. Cathy Chan

4. John Lowe
5. Mike Perez
6. Alan Walker

Listen for it

People say *By the way* . . . to change the topic of a conversation.

B Listen again and check your answers.

6

A Match each statement or question with the best response.

1. Hello, Leanne.
2. This is Alan Walker.
3. Are you Paul King?
4. I'm Cathy Chan.

- Hi, I'm Mike Perez.
- No, I'm John Lowe.
- Nice to meet you, Alan.
- Hi, Tony.

B Listen and check your answers.

7

Listen and circle the answers that are right for you.

1.	Yes, I am.	No, I'm not.	4.	Yes, I am.	No, I'm not.
2.	Yes, it is.	No, it isn't.	5.	Yes, it is.	No, it isn't.
3.	Yes, I am.	No, I'm not.	6.	Yes, I do.	No, I don't.

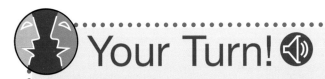

Your Turn! 🔊

Making introductions

Sample Dialog

A: Hi, my name's Tony Kim.
B: Pleased to meet you, Tony. I'm Yumiko Sato.
A: Sorry, your name is Yumiko? How do you spell that?
B: It's Y-U-M-I-K-O. And my last name is Sato. S-A-T-O.
A: Nice to meet you, Yumiko. Are you a friend of John's?
B: No, I'm a friend of Leanne's.

Useful Expressions

- How do you do, Wendy?
- Excuse me, are you Paul King?
- No, I'm John Lowe.
- Do you know Cathy Chan?
- Are you a student?
- Are you from Japan?

Try this . . .

Introduce yourself to three classmates. Find out at least two pieces of information about each one.

Name: _____ Information: _____

Name: _____ Information: _____

Name: _____ Information: _____

In Focus: *Questions for a first meeting*

It's not unusual to ask questions to find out about someone when meeting for the first time. In some countries, there are certain questions that you shouldn't ask because they might make the person uncomfortable. *In your country, what types of questions are OK to ask on first meeting someone? What types of questions are not OK?*

> In Korea, it's OK to ask someone's age so you know whether to use formal language.

> In Canada, it's not OK to ask someone's age because some people don't like to say how old they are.

> In Mexico, it's not OK to ask about someone's religion because some people think it's too personal.

This is my family.

Goals | • Identifying family members

1

A **Look at the family tree and complete the sentences below.**

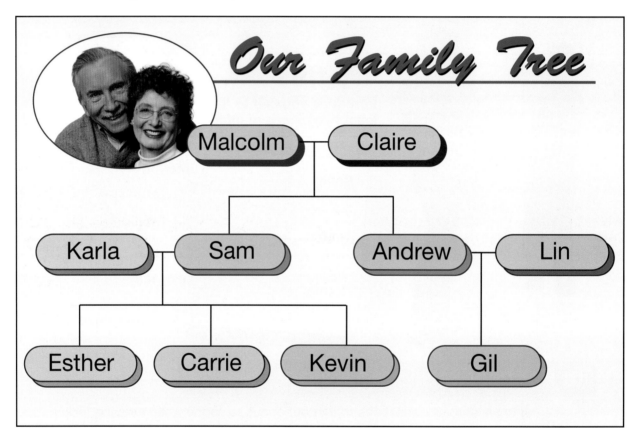

Our Family Tree

Malcolm — Claire

Karla — Sam   Andrew — Lin

Esther   Carrie   Kevin   Gil

1. _____ is _____ husband, Sam's father, and _____ grandfather.

2. _____ is Karla's daughter and _____ sister.

3. _____ is _____ mother and Kevin's grandmother.

4. _____ is Andrew's brother and _____ uncle.

5. _____ is _____ son and Andrew's nephew.

6. _____ is Sam's wife and _____ aunt.

7. _____ is _____ grandson and Gil's cousin.

8. _____ is Claire's granddaughter and _____ niece.

B **Brainstorm! Work with a partner. Can you think of any other ways that the people are related? Write some more sentences.**

A **Listen. How is the speaker related to each person? Circle the correct answer.**

1. Jon is the speaker's (son / brother).

2. Darren is the speaker's (uncle / father).

3. Sara is the speaker's (niece / granddaughter).

4. Lily is the speaker's (cousin / sister).

5. Rob is the speaker's (nephew / grandson).

B **Listen again and check your answers.**

A **Listen. You will hear four people talking about their families. Number the pictures (1–4) in the order you hear them described.**

B **Listen again. How many people can you identify? Label each photo with the correct names.**

Nicole   Doug   Claire   Sherry   Richard

Erin   Ellen   Michael   Jodie   Leslie

4

A Listen. Is the final sound of each word /s/ or /z/? Write each word next to the correct sound.

1. sisters	3. aunts	5. brothers	7. parents	9. husbands
2. cousins	4. students	6. sons	8. grandmothers	10. teachers

/s/	
/z/	

B Listen again and check your answers. Practice saying the words.

5

Listen for it

Wow! is an informal way of saying you're surprised or impressed.

A Listen to Naomi. Then read the statements and circle *True* or *False*.

1.	Naomi is from Japan.	True	False
2.	She is talking about her own family.	True	False
3.	One daughter's name is Setsuko.	True	False
4.	The son's name is Kazuo.	True	False
6.	Naomi is going to Tokyo.	True	False

B Listen again and complete the family tree.

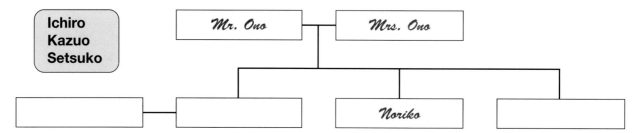

Ichiro
Kazuo
Setsuko

Mr. Ono — Mrs. Ono

Noriko

6

Listen and circle the answers that are right for you.

1. Yes	No	3. Yes	No	5. Yes	No
2. Yes	No	4. Yes	No	6. Yes	No

# Your Turn! 🔊

Talking about your family

A: Here are my mother and father and down here are my sisters and me.
B: Are you the oldest?
A: No, both of my sisters are older. Caitlin is 25 and Vanessa is 22.
B: So these are their husbands?
A: Yes, Caitlin is married to Steve and that's their son Jamie.
B: What about Vanessa?
A: Vanessa is married but she and her husband don't have any children yet.

Useful Expressions

- How many people are there in your family?
- Is this your brother's wife?
- What's your nephew's name?
- Are you the oldest or the youngest?
- I'm the middle child.
- I have one older brother and two younger sisters.

Try this . . . Make a rough sketch of your family tree. Show a partner your sketch and answer questions about your family. Now, switch roles.

In Focus: *Celebrity families*

Royal families around the world hold a great fascination for the public, perhaps because they represent the style and elegance of a bygone era. These days, celebrity families like the members of corporate dynasties, the families of movie stars, and even TV families such as 'The Simpsons' are the focus of intense media attention. *Who are some famous families in your country? Can you name all of the members and explain the relationships between them?*

Former U.S. President John F. Kennedy's parents' names were Joseph and Rose. His wife's name was Jacqueline and his children were Caroline, John, Jr. and Patrick.

Britain's Prince William and his younger brother Prince Henry, whose nickname is Harry, are the sons of Charles, Prince of Wales, and the late Diana Spencer, Princess of Wales.

UNIT 3

He's the one in the blue shirt.

Goals • Identifying people through physical description

1

A Look at the picture and use the words in the box to describe each person.

- She/He is . . . young middle-aged old
- Her/his hair is . . . black brown blond(e) red grey
- Her/his eyes are . . . brown blue green
- She/He is . . . tall average height short
- She/He is . . . heavyset average build thin
- She/He has (a) . . . long hair short hair mustache beard
- She/He is wearing (a) . . . hat glasses jacket shirt skirt necktie

B **Brainstorm!** Think of some other ways to describe people. Work with a partner and write at least three sentences to describe someone that you know.

20

2

A **Listen. You will hear a conversation about the five people listed below. Look at the picture and draw lines from the names to the correct people.**

Cindy Carlyle

Charles Markham

Elaine Nolan

Tony Tan

Alan Watts

Listen for it

Um . . . or *Uh* . . . are used when you are deciding or still unsure what to say next.

B **Listen again and check your answers.**

3

A **Listen to short descriptions of each of the people in Task 2 and number the names (1–5).**

____ Cindy Carlyle   ____ Tony Tan   ____ Charles Markham

____ Alan Watts   ____ Elaine Nolan

B **Listen again and check your answers.**

He's the one in the blue shirt.   **21**

4

A Listen. Who are the people describing? Number the pictures (1–5).

☐
• mother
• daughter

☐
• uncle
• father

☐
• sister
• daughter

☐
• nephew
• brother

☐
• cousin
• mother

B What is the relationship of each person to the speaker? Listen again and circle the correct answers.

5

A Is it a question or a statement? Listen to the examples.

Example 1: He's the managing director? (↗)   **Example 2:** He's the managing director. (↘)

Now listen and circle the correct answer.

1. Question Statement	**3.** Question Statement	**5.** Question Statement
2. Question Statement	**4.** Question Statement	**6.** Question Statement

B Listen again and practice.

6

Listen and circle the answers that are right for you.

1. Yes, I am. No, I'm not.	**3.** Yes, it is. No, it isn't.	**5.** Yes, I do. No, I don't.
2. Yes, I do. No, I don't.	**4.** Yes, I am. No, I'm not.	**6.** Yes, I am. No, I'm not.

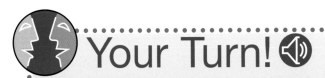# Your Turn! 🔊

Describing someone's appearance

Sample Dialog

A: The person I'm describing has brown hair and blue eyes.
B: Is the person's hair long or short?
A: Not too long. I guess you'd say it's shoulder length.
B: Is the person tall or short?
A: I'd say average height. But the person is a bit heavyset.
B: Is the person wearing glasses?
A: No, but he's wearing blue jeans and a brown shirt.

Useful Expressions

- What is he wearing?
- Would you say he's middle-aged?
- What color is her hair?
- Does he have a mustache or beard?
- Is she holding a purse?
- What color shirt is he wearing?
- You mean the young, blond guy over there?

Pair Work . . .

Write a brief description of a classmate in the space. Then, describe and answer questions about the person. Have your partner decide which classmate you're talking about.

In Focus: *The ideal look*

Different cultures have different ideals of beauty for both women and men. In many parts of the world 'thin is in,' whereas people in other parts of the world prefer a more full-bodied appearance. *What physical characteristics define the ideal man and woman in your country? Name some of the people who fit this description.*

To me, Chinese actress Gong Li is perfect because she's beautiful and smart.

The things that make Brad Pitt so sexy are his blue eyes and great smile.

Some people think supermodels are perfect but I think they're too thin.

He's the one in the blue shirt.

Do you like rock?

Goals • Identifying likes/dislikes and preferences
• Identifying different genres of music

1

A **Look at the photos. Who are the people? What type of music does each person sing or play?**

B **What do you think about these kinds of music? Check (✔) your answers, then share them with a partner.**

Kind of music	Love	Like	Don't mind	Don't like	Can't stand
Jazz					
Pop					
Rock					
Classical					
Other: _____					

C **Brainstorm!** Work with a partner. How many kinds of music can you name? Make a list. Think of a singer or musician for each.

2

 A Listen to each conversation and check (✔) the CD
Mick and Marsha talk about.

❶

The Pink Bicycle

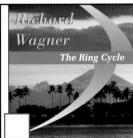
Richard Wagner — *The Ring Cycle*

❷

Dude Band — *Hot & Wild*

Two Bad — *Hard-Wired*

❸

Lee Zane — *Zoom to You*

Leah Shane — *Room to Move*

❹

Edgar Oates — *Big Easy*

Big Eddy Rhodes — *Speakeasy*

B Listen again. Does Marsha like or dislike each CD? Circle or .

3

 A Listen to the example. Then listen and circle the word that is stressed in each sentence.

Ex. I like classical.

1. No, it's jazz that I like.

2. I like it.

3. No, but my girlfriend does.

4. Classical music? I can't stand it!

5. It's OK, but I prefer rock.

B Listen again and practice.

4

A Listen to the conversation about the Big Audio Awards. Which singers are nominated for Best New Artist? Check (✔) the names.

Listen for it

You're kidding! is an informal way of expressing surprise or disbelief.

☐ Kelly King   ☐ Jenny Hernandez   ☐ Li'l Stevie

☐ Tommy Devlin   ☐ Aki Matsumura

B Listen again. Which singers does Randy like? Circle them.

5

A Listen to the radio broadcast. What does the DJ talk about? Check (✔) the correct answer.

☐ The winners of the Big Audio Awards.

☐ The nominations for the Big Audio Awards.

☐ His choices for the Big Audio Awards.

B Listen again. Fill in the blanks with information from the box.

| 1. Most Wanted | 3. jazz | 5. Kelly King | 7. rock |
| 2. Street Fight | 4. pop | 6. Rough & Smooth | 8. Sam White |

Award Category	Performer	Title	Kind of Music
Best Song	_____	Love Me Silly	_____
Best Album	The Glory Hounds	_____	_____
Best Video	_____	_____	rap
Best Soundtrack	_____	The Other Side of Five	_____

6

Listen and circle the answers that are right for you.

1. Yes, I do.   No, I don't.   I don't know much about it.

2. I like it.   I don't mind it.   I don't like it.

3. Rock.   Pop.   Neither.

4. A lot of different kinds.   Just a few kinds.   Just one or two kinds.

5. I like her songs.   I don't really like her songs.   I don't know many of her songs.

6. I listen to it a lot.   I sometimes listen to it.   I never listen to it.

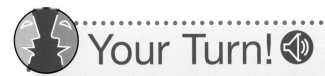

Your Turn! 🔊

Talking about music preferences

Sample Dialog

A: Hey, Jeff, do you like U2?
B: Oh yeah. They're fantastic!
A: What's your favorite song?
B: Let me think . . . I really like 'Sunday Bloody Sunday.'
A: Oh really? I prefer 'I Still Haven't Found What I'm Looking For.'

Useful Expressions

- Who's your favorite singer?
- What kind of music do you like?
- I really like jazz.
- Me too. What do you think of Miles Davis?
- How do you feel about rap?
- I don't mind it, but I prefer rock.

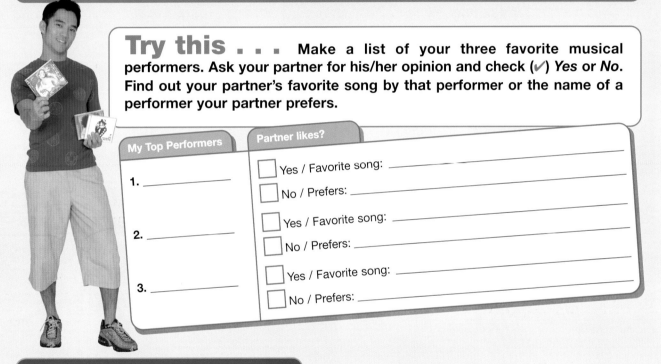

Try this . . . Make a list of your three favorite musical performers. Ask your partner for his/her opinion and check (✔) *Yes* or *No*. Find out your partner's favorite song by that performer or the name of a performer your partner prefers.

My Top Performers	Partner likes?
1. _____	☐ Yes / Favorite song: _____ ☐ No / Prefers: _____
2. _____	☐ Yes / Favorite song: _____ ☐ No / Prefers: _____
3. _____	☐ Yes / Favorite song: _____ ☐ No / Prefers: _____

In Focus: *Music legends*

Many musicians worldwide have earned awards for their career accomplishments. In the United States, winners of the Grammy Award for Lifetime Achievement include pop star John Lennon, opera singer Enrico Caruso, and jazz great Ella Fitzgerald. *Which musical performers in your country deserve awards for lifetime achievement? Give reasons.*

Cho Yong-pil is the biggest star in Korea. He started singing about 40 years ago.

Everyone knows the Beatles. They're the most famous group ever.

Antonio Carlos Jobim was Brazil's greatest jazz composer. Musicians still play his songs today.

It's a really interesting place.

Goals | • Understanding descriptions of places

1

A Look at the real estate brochures and use the words below to describe each area.

| big | beautiful | quiet | inexpensive |

| exciting | safe | modern | relaxing |

Settle in Smallville

LIFE IN THE CITY

Seaside Paradise

Suburban LIVING

B Match each word from the task above with one with the opposite meaning.

big small   _____ traditional   _____ ugly   _____ boring

_____ noisy   _____ dangerous   _____ stressful   _____ expensive

C **Brainstorm!** Can you think of any other words to describe cities? Work with a partner and make a list. What words would you use to describe the place where you live?

2

A
Listen to the conversations and number the pictures (1–3).

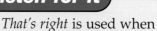

Listen for it

That's right is used when you remember something or are reminded of it.

B
Where does each person work now? Listen again and match the names to the cities.

1. Alan
2. John
3. Chanaboon
4. Kelvin
5. Mark
6. Pam
7. Greta

- Jakarta
- Taipei
- Singapore
- Bangkok
- San Francisco
- Hong Kong
- New York

3

A
Listen. Which of the underlined sounds are the same? Join the words with a line.

1. Malay<u>s</u>ian   3. Chine<u>s</u>e   5. Egyp<u>t</u>ian

2. A<u>s</u>ian   4. Bra<u>z</u>ilian   6. Rus<u>s</u>ian

B
Listen again and practice.

It's a really interesting place.   **29**

4

A

Listen and check (✔) the places you hear.

> **Listen for it**
>
> *Uh-huh* is an informal way of saying *yes* or expressing understanding.

✔ Chicago	_____ New York	_____ Singapore	_____ Bangkok
_____ Miami	_____ Tokyo	_____ Denver	_____ Seoul

B

Listen again. How does Dave describe each city? Match each adjective with the correct city.

interesting	_____	exciting	_____
big	_____	clean	_____
safe	_____	modern	_____
convenient	_____	inexpensive	_____

5

Listen and circle the answers that are right for you.

1. Yes, I am.	No, I'm not.	**4.** Yes, I am.	No, I'm not.
2. Yes, I did.	No, I didn't.	**5.** Yes, I do.	No, I don't.
3. Yes, it is.	No, it isn't.	**6.** Yes, I am.	No, I'm not.

Your Turn! 🔊

Describing what places are like

Sample Dialog

A: Which city do you most want to visit?
B: I really want to see Paris.
A: Oh yeah? Why do you want to go there?
B: Well, it seems like a really exciting place.
A: What would you like to do there?
B: I'd love to visit the Eiffel Tower and go to the Louvre. I've heard Paris is pretty expensive, though.
A: Yeah, but I'm sure you'd enjoy it.

Useful Expressions

- What's Tokyo like?
- It's very big and modern.
- Have you ever been to Hong Kong?
- Yes. It's an interesting city but very crowded.
- Is Los Angeles a safe place to live?
- What is there to see and do there?

Try this . . .

Think of three cities you would like to visit. Tell your partner. Ask questions about the cities your partner chose.

My partner's top 3 cities

1. _____
Why? _____
2. _____
Why? _____
3. _____
Why? _____

In Focus: *World-class cities*

Cities around the world compete to hold prestigious international events like the Olympic Games and the soccer World Cup. Many people think that hosting such an event gives a city 'world-class' status. *How would you describe the city where you live? Would people outside your country consider it a 'world-class' city? Why or why not?*

Montreal is a really exciting city. Sometimes it's a bit noisy, though.

I think Bangkok is a world-class city but it's also very crowded.

My hometown is quite small but it's a beautiful place to live.

Review

1

A Listen and circle the names you hear.

Jane	Rick	Jim	Tina	Jenny
Mike	Rita	Nick	Rena	Dick

B Listen again and number the pictures (1–4). One picture is extra.

2

A Anne is identifying some people at a party. Match the names to the relationship words.

Name	Relationship	Description
Harry •	• cousin	• heavyset
Judy •	• aunt	• wearing glasses
Kevin •	• grandmother	• tall
Anne •	• brother	• red shirt
Lyle •	• father	• beard

B Listen again. Match the relationship words to the descriptions.

32

3

A **Listen to the radio broadcast and complete the chart.**

Country	No. 1 Song	Singer/Group
England	_____	Fourfold
Ireland	Strength in Numbers	_____
_____	Fired Up	Kenny Isaacs
_____	_____	The Blazers

B **Listen again and check your answers.**

4

A **Listen and circle the best answer.**

1. Jiro visited Canada . . .
   a. for a business meeting.
   b. to study English.
   c. to visit his family.

2. He went to the top of the . . .
   a. Calgary Tower.
   b. Cabot Tower.
   c. CN Tower.

3. His favorite city is . . .
   a. Toronto.
   b. Vancouver.
   c. Banff.

B **Listen again. Circle the words Jiro uses to describe each city.**

Vancouver

Toronto

Banff

| expensive | boring | modern | quiet | traditional | beautiful |
| exciting | safe | big | relaxing | stressful | small |

5

Listen and circle the answers that are right for you.

1. Great!
So-so.
Not too good.

2. None.
One.
More than one.

3. Tall.
Average height.
Short.

4. I like it.
I don't listen to it.
I don't like it.

5. Exciting.
Average.
Boring.

Review Units 1–5 **33**

UNIT 6

This is where I live.

Goals | • Understanding descriptions of homes

1

A **Look at the photos of rooms in a house. Use the words in the box to complete the real estate advertisement.**

kitchen	bedroom	dining room	bathroom	living room

For Sale or Rent Lakeside Estates

★ Fully furnished one- and two-_____ homes.

★ Spacious _____ for relaxing, _____ for meals, and modern _____ with all-new appliances. _____ with basin and old-fashioned bathtub.

★ Very bright rooms and great views.

★ Close to public transportation and shopping.

★ Parking available.

Tel: 555-3819

B **Use the words in the box to complete the sentences about the house.**

sofa	table	range	bed	chairs	refrigerator	windows
doors	balcony	cabinet	armchair	microwave	cupboard	coffee table

1. The kitchen has a _____, _____, _____, and _____.

2. The bedroom includes a double _____ and a _____ overlooking the lake.

3. There's a _____, _____, and _____ in the living room.

4. The dining room has a _____, five _____, and a large _____.

5. Large _____ and French-style _____ make every room warm and bright.

C **Brainstorm! Work with a partner. Think of some other common household furnishings. Where would you put them in the rooms above?**

2

A Read the statements. Then listen and circle *True* or *False*.

1. Haruko is talking to a real estate agent.   True   False

2. She is showing the other person some photographs.   True   False

3. She has rented a house.   True   False

4. Her new place is in Tokyo.   True   False

5. Her favorite room is the bedroom.   True   False

B Listen again and check (✔) Haruko's favorite room.

3

A Listen to the real estate ads. Are they for houses or apartments?
Are the places for sale or for rent? Circle the correct answers.

1. House / Apartment   Sale / Rent

2. House / Apartment   Sale / Rent

3. House / Apartment   Sale / Rent

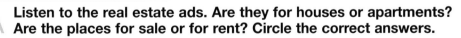

Listen for it

Go on is a way to urge someone to do something.

B Listen again and check your answers.

4

A Listen to the dialog and check (✔) the correct answer.

☐ Kelly is talking to a real estate agency on Bonham Road.

☐ Kelly is looking for an apartment on Bonham Road.

☐ Kelly is looking for an apartment similar to one on Bonham Road.

> **Listen for it**
>
> *Sounds great* is an informal way of expressing satisfaction or finalizing plans.

B Listen again and check (✔) the correct apartment.

Kitchen

Dining

Living   Bedroom

Bedroom   Bedroom

Dining

Kitchen

Living

Bedroom   Bedroom

Study

Living   Kitchen

Dining

Balcony   Living   Bedroom

Kitchen

Dining

5

A Listen and underline the words with the same sound as *th* in *there*. Circle the words with the same sound as *th* in *three*.

1. There are three apartments in the paper for rent.

2. They said we can find our way with this map.

3. Are these the things we need for the apartment?

B Add at least two other words to each list and practice.

There, the, _____   Three, thirty, _____

6

Listen and circle the answers that are right for you.

1. A house.	An apartment.	4. Rent.	Own.
2. Yes, it does.	No, it doesn't.	5. Yes, there is.	No, there isn't.
3. Yes, I do.	No, I don't.	6. Yes, I do.	No, I don't.

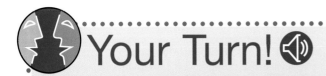
Your Turn! 🔊

Describing an apartment

Sample Dialog

A: How many rooms does the apartment have?
B: Six. There are two bedrooms, two bathrooms, a living room, and a kitchen.
A: What furnishings are there in the living room?
B: It has a sofa, an armchair, and a bookcase.
A: Does the living room have a TV?
B: No, but there's one in the each bedroom. The living room also has a balcony overlooking the city.

Useful Expressions

• Does the apartment come with a washer and dryer?
• Do both bathrooms have showers?
• How much is the monthly rent?
• It's $650 a month plus utilities.
• What floor is the apartment on?

Try this . . .

You are looking for someone to rent your home. Make a list of the rooms and furnishings. Tell your partner and answer any questions. Then, switch roles.

In Focus: *Home sweet home*

In many parts of the world, it's a custom to hold a 'housewarming' party shortly after you move into a new home. Party guests typically bring gifts for the person holding the party and are treated to a meal and a tour of the new home. According to tradition, the friendship of the guests 'warms' the house, making the new occupants feel even more comfortable in their new home. *What are the customs associated with finding or moving into a new home in your country?*

New homeowners in my country sometimes ask a priest to hold a ceremony to bless their house.

Kitchenware or bottles of wine are among the most common housewarming gifts in my country.

It's important to make sure the house has the proper *feng shui*, or harmony between various elements like doorways and staircases.

It's on the third floor.

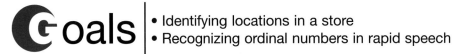

Goals • Identifying locations in a store
• Recognizing ordinal numbers in rapid speech

1

A **Look at the sale signs. Write the correct floor number for each sale.**

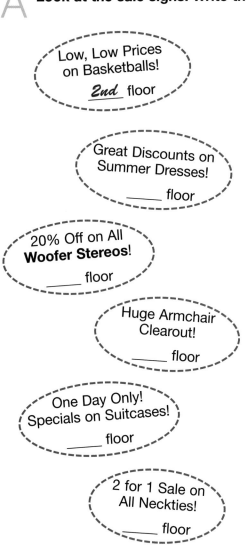

Low, Low Prices
on Basketballs!
_2nd_ floor

Great Discounts on
Summer Dresses!
_____ floor

20% Off on All
Woofer Stereos!
_____ floor

Huge Armchair
Clearout!
_____ floor

One Day Only!
Specials on Suitcases!
_____ floor

2 for 1 Sale on
All Neckties!
_____ floor

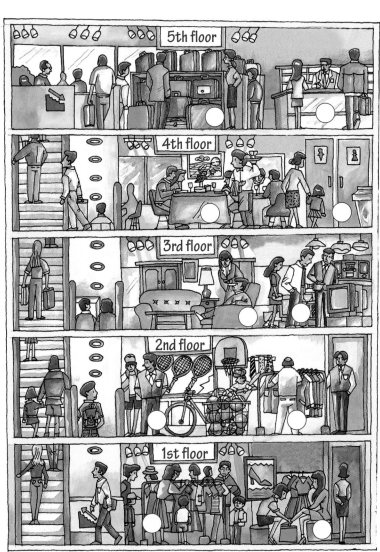

B **Now, use the words in the box to label the departments and other areas of Maxwell's Superstore. Write the correct numbers in the circles.**

1. cashier	3. children's wear	5. electrical goods	7. furniture	9. luggage
2. men's wear	4. restaurant	6. restrooms	8. sporting goods	10. women's wear

C **Brainstorm! Work with a partner. Think of at least one more item you could find in each of the departments you labeled. Can you think of any other departments you might find in a department store?**

2

A Complete the following sentences with *in*, *on*, *next to*, or *between*.

   1. Men's wear is _____ the second floor.

   2. CD players are _____ the electrical goods department.

   3. The electrical goods department is _____ the furniture department.

   4. Tennis rackets are _____ the second floor in sporting goods.

   5. Sporting goods is _____ the restaurant and the escalator.

B **Listen and check your answers.**

3

A **Listen to the elevator announcements. Write the correct floor number for each picture.**

1. . . . track suits, *tennis rackets*, soccer balls, roller blades, and _____ . . .

2. . . . _____, shorts, _____, _____, and hats . . .

3. . . . _____, VCRs, _____, microwaves, and MD players . . .

4. . . . sofas, _____, chairs, _____, and _____ . . .

B **Listen again and complete the lists below each picture.**

4

A **Listen and circle the number you hear.**

1. second	seventh	**4.** first	fourth
2. eight	eighth	**5.** nine	ninth
3. sixth	six	**6.** thirteen	thirteenth

B **Listen again and practice.**

It's on the third floor.   **39**

5

A Listen to the public address announcement and label the missing departments at Shoprite Discount Warehouse.

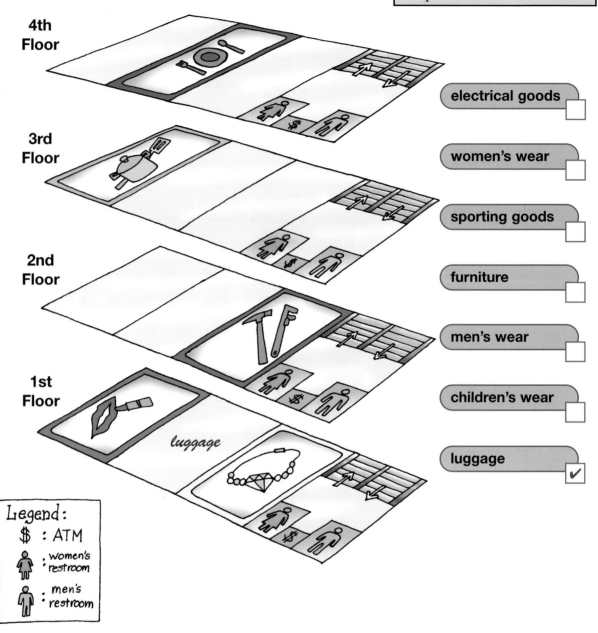

4th Floor

3rd Floor

2nd Floor

1st Floor

electrical goods ☐

women's wear ☐

sporting goods ☐

furniture ☐

men's wear ☐

children's wear ☐

luggage ✔

luggage

Legend:
$: ATM
👩 : women's restroom
👨 : men's restroom

B Listen again and check (✔) the departments where there are special offers.

6

Look at the floor plan in Task 5 and listen. Circle the correct answers.

1. True	False	**3.** True	False	**5.** True	False
2. True	False	**4.** True	False	**6.** True	False

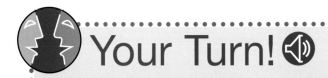

Your Turn! 🔊

Talking about locations in a store

Sample Dialog

A: Can I help you?
B: Yes, I'm looking for running shoes.
A: Running shoes? Right over there in the sporting goods department.
B: Great. I'm also looking for a skirt for my wife.
A: OK. Women's wear is on the third floor next to the children's wear department. You can take the escalator.
B: And where's that?
A: Right next to hardware.

Useful Expressions

- Excuse me. Can you tell me where to find CD players?
- Sure. They're right upstairs in the electrical goods department.
- Take the escalator to four and it's right next to the food court.
- What floor is sporting goods on?
- Is there a restroom on this floor?

Try this . . .

Write the names of five friends or family members and think of a gift you'd like to buy for each person. Tell a partner what you're looking for. Ask where you can find each item at Shoprite Discount Warehouse.

Gift List

Name	Gift
1.	
2.	
3.	
4.	
5.	

In Focus: *You better shop around*

In many countries, traditional open-air markets, such as Namdaemun in Korea or Singapore's Clarke Quay flea market, compete with shopping centers and department stores for customers. *Have you ever been to a traditional market in your country? What are some advantages of shopping at open-air markets versus department stores? What are some disadvantages?*

In Thailand, traditional markets have much lower prices than department stores.

North American department stores offer better quality products than open-air markets.

Open-air markets in Mexico have a wider selection than shopping malls.

It's on the third floor.

UNIT 8

Can you work weekends?

Goals • Identifying abilities
• Identifying preferences

A What's the ideal job for you? Complete the survey below.

Career Survey

Use the scale to rate how important each item is to you.

	Not Important					Very Important
1. Being part of a team	0	1	2	3	4	5
2. Working in a stress-free environment	0	1	2	3	4	5
3. Meeting lots of people	0	1	2	3	4	5
4. Working with technology	0	1	2	3	4	5
5. Creating new things	0	1	2	3	4	5
6. Working for a big company	0	1	2	3	4	5
7. Using my language skills	0	1	2	3	4	5
8. Having control over others	0	1	2	3	4	5
9. Earning a high salary	0	1	2	3	4	5
10. Helping people	0	1	2	3	4	5
11. Working with my hands	0	1	2	3	4	5
12. Having opportunities to travel	0	1	2	3	4	5
13. Working in an office	0	1	2	3	4	5

B Look at your partner's answers. Would your partner be suitable for these occupations? Why or why not? What would be the ideal job for your partner?

airline pilot	store owner	journalist	salesperson
business manager	TV producer	teacher	police officer
mechanic	doctor	computer programmer	social worker

C **Brainstorm!** Work with a partner. Think of at least three more occupations. What sorts of skills and personal qualities are needed to do these jobs? Make a list.

2

A **Listen to the four conversations and number the occupations (1–4).**

Listen for it

Right? is used to check that someone understands and agrees with you.

B **Listen again. How does each person describe the job? Circle the correct word.**

1. creative

   interesting

2. dangerous

   boring

3. stressful

   enjoyable

4. high-paying

   satisfying

3

A **Listen to the questions and circle the best responses.**

1. It's 555-1136.   It's 457 11th St.

2. I went to Stanford.   I want to go to Stanford.

3. No, but I can speak Korean.   No, I'm Japanese.

4. I'm the senior sales manager.   I was the senior sales manager.

5. I was there for about five years.   I left there about five years ago.

B **Listen again and check your answers.**

4

A **Which words are stressed? Listen to the example. Then listen and underline the stressed words.**

Ex. Can you speak <u>English</u>?

1. I can speak Spanish.

2. I can't drive a truck.

3. Can you work weekends?

4. Yes, I can.

5. John can use PictureShop, can't he?

B **Listen again and practice.**

5

A
Read the job ad. Then listen to the two job interviews. Write *Yes* or *No* for each item on the interview form.

WANTED

Paris-based fashion/lifestyle magazine seeks experienced designer to supervise layout and design team. Computer design skills essential. Must be bilingual.

Email résumé to
editor@fashionparis.co.fr

Job Interview Form

	Patricia	Julian
• Can use DesignWiz software	_____	_____
• Can take professional photos	_____	_____
• Can speak and write French	_____	_____
• Can type 60 words per minute	_____	_____
• Can work with spreadsheets	_____	_____
• Can work weekends	_____	_____
• Can travel overseas	_____	_____

B
Listen again and check your answers. Who do think is the best candidate for the job? Share your opinion with a partner.

6

Listen and circle the answers that are right for you.

1. Yes, I do.	No, I don't.	**4.** Yes, it is.	No, it isn't.
2. Yes, I have.	No, I haven't.	**5.** Yes, I do.	No, I don't.
3. Yes, I can.	No, I can't.	**6.** Yes, I am.	No, I'm not.

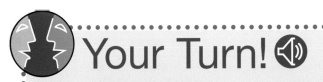

Your Turn! 🔊

Asking and answering job interview questions

Sample Dialog

A: We're looking for someone with computer design skills.

B: I can use DesignWiz software. I also know PictureShop.

A: OK. Can you work with spreadsheets?

B: Yes, I used spreadsheets in my previous job.

A: What about your language skills? Can you speak French?

B: Yes, I can. I studied in France for three years. I love to travel.

A: That's great. I just have a few more questions.

Useful Expressions

- Why did you leave your last job?
- I was looking for a new challenge.
- Why do you think you're the best candidate for the job?
- I have a lot of experience and I'm very hardworking.
- Are you willing to travel or move to another city?
- Yes, I love to travel and I'd be willing to relocate.

Try this . . .

Work with a partner. Role-play the job interview in Task 5. Take notes on your partner's job qualifications. Switch roles.

Job Interview Form

Personal qualities: _____

Job skills: _____

Language skills: _____

Availability: _____

In Focus: *Prestigious careers*

Respondents to a 2001 survey by the Harris Poll, a U.S. market research and consulting firm, named doctors, teachers, and scientists as the three most prestigious professions from a list of seventeen. The three least prestigious jobs were banker, accountant, and businessperson. *What are the most prestigious professions in your country? What are the least prestigious? Why do you think people respect certain professions over others?*

I think teachers get a lot of prestige because it's such a difficult job.

Politicians don't get any respect in my country. People think they're dishonest.

I think nurses deserve more respect because they work so hard.

Where's the ferry terminal?

 Goals | • Identifying locations in a city
• Understanding directions

1

A Read the statements (1–5). Use the information in the brochure to decide which hotel each statement describes.

1. It's close to a major shopping center.

_____

2. It's across from a ferry terminal.

_____

3. It's near several movie theaters.

_____

4. It's between two subway stations.

_____

5. It's beside a zoo.

_____

Welcome to Hong Kong!

Make the most of your stay by booking into one of these popular downtown hotels.

Luxury

Mandarin Oriental *5 Connaught Rd., Central.* Conveniently located opposite the Star Ferry Terminal.

Conrad Hong Kong *88 Queensway, Admiralty.* Just by the Conrad is Pacific Place, one of Hong Kong's largest shopping complexes.

Park Lane *310 Gloucester Rd., Causeway.* Located beside Victoria Park, close to the Pearl, Jade, and Windsor Cinemas.

Mid-range

Eaton Hotel Hong Kong *380 Nathan Rd., Yaumatei.* Just a short walk from Jordan MTR station to the south and Yaumatei MTR station to the north.

Budget

YWCA Garden View International House *1 Macdonnell Rd., Mid Levels, Hong Kong Island.* Located next to the Zoological & Botanical Gardens, home to hundreds of different kinds of birds and animals.

B Underline the parts of the hotel descriptions that helped you decide.

C **Brainstorm!** Work with a partner. Think of a building in your area. List as many ways as you can to describe its location.

2

A Listen to the conversations. What does each person want to see or do? Number the photos (1–6).

Got it is an informal way of saying that you understand something.

Pacific Place
Times Square

Victoria Harbour
Aberdeen Harbour

Hong Kong Arts Centre
Hong Kong Cultural Centre

King's Park
Kowloon Park

Tin Hau Temple
Man Mo Temple

Citibank Plaza
Bank of America Tower

B Listen again. Where is each person advised to go? Circle the correct answers.

3

A Read the statements and listen to the directions. Circle *T* for *True* or *F* for *False*.

1. The drugstore is across from the church. **T F**
2. The hotel is in front of the bookstore. **T F**
3. The market is next to the hospital. **T F**
4. The hotel is on Kensington Street. **T F**
5. The supermarket is across from the mall. **T F**

B Listen again and check your answers.

4

A Listen. Does the intonation rise or fall at the end of each question. Circle ⌒ or ⌄.

1. Do you know where the station is? ⌒ ⌄
2. When does the bus get here? ⌒ ⌄
3. Is there a bookstore nearby? ⌒ ⌄
4. How do I get to the ferry terminal? ⌒ ⌄
5. Where is the drugstore? ⌒ ⌄
6. Are there any banks around here? ⌒ ⌄

B Listen again and practice.

Where's the ferry terminal?   **47**

5

 A **Listen to the tourist information about Kowloon. Number the places in the order that you hear them (1–6).**

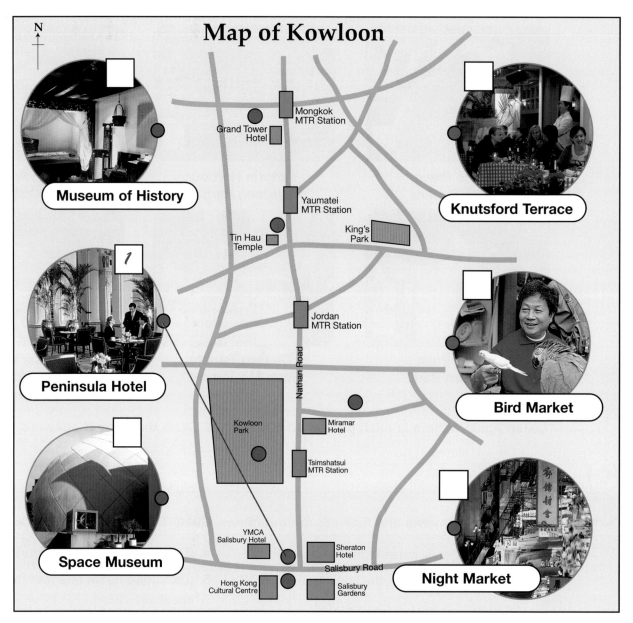

B **Listen again. Draw lines between each place and its location on the map.**

6

 Listen and circle the answers that are right for you.

1. Yes, there is.   No, there isn't.   4. Yes, I do.   No, I don't.

2. Yes, I do.   No, I don't.   5. Yes, you can.   No, you can't

3. Yes, it is.   No, it isn't.   6. Yes, there are.   No, there aren't.

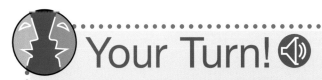

Your Turn! 🔊

Asking for directions and describing locations

Sample Dialog

A: Excuse me, I'm looking for a good place to have dinner with friends. Could you recommend a place?

B: The best choice is probably Knutsford Terrace. It isn't too far from here.

A: Knutsford Terrace? Could you tell me where that is?

B: Sure. It's on Kimberley Road, close to the Miramar.

A: Sorry. I don't know where the Miramar is.

B: Oh, it's on Nathan Road, across from Kowloon Park.

A: Close to the Miramar Hotel, across from Kowloon Park. Thanks.

Useful Expressions

- Excuse me, is there a post office near here?
- Sure. Go up Nathan Road to Middle Road and turn right.
- Is the Causeway Centre in Kowloon?
- No, it's not. It's in Wanchai.
- Is it within walking distance from here?
- No, you should probably take a cab.

Try this . . . **Work with a partner. Think of three things you'd like to do in Kowloon. Ask your partner to recommend some places and give you directions. Take notes in the space below.**

In Focus: *It's a must-see*

Travel companies sometimes offer tours built around particular themes like historical sites, cultural institutions, or popular nightspots. *Which places in your city would you include on a tour of important historical sites? Which places are 'must-see' stops on a cultural tour of your city? Where would you take tourists who wanted to visit the best nightspots?*

Visitors to Tokyo can learn about Japanese culture in the museums at Ueno-koen Park.

The National Palace is a 'must-see' in Mexico City. The murals there show Mexico's history.

Soho is the main nightlife area in London. You can find all the best pubs and nightclubs there.

How does it work?

Goals | • Understanding instructions
• Following sequence of events

1

A Look at the instruction manuals and use the words in the box to label the pictures.

(MD Player)   (DVD Player)   (Digital Camera)   (Computer)

- User's Manual for IGN A520 Series® _____

- Getting to Know Your Tunemaster® _____

- How to Use the Vidtronic™ _____

- FotoMate® _____: Operating Instructions

B Write the correct instruction under each picture (1–8).

Instructions
(Put in)
(Open)
(Press)
(Adjust)
(Turn on)
(Plug in)
(Click)
(Move)

1. _____

2. _____

3. _____

4. _____

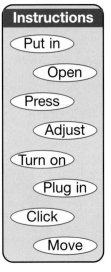

5. _____

6. _____

7. _____

8. _____

C Brainstorm! What other words can you use to talk about a computer? Make a list.

2

A **Listen and circle the words you hear in each conversation.**

1.	Press	Put in	Click	Move	Open	Adjust	Close	Plug in

2.	Press	Put in	Move	Open	Close	Adjust	Turn on	Take out

3.	Press	Put in	Click	Move	Open	Plug in	Turn on	Take out

B **Listen again. Which item is each person talking about? Number the photos (1–3).**

3

A **Gerald is calling a Help Line for instructions on how to use his MD Player. Listen. What instructions does he get? Write *Do* or *Don't* in the space next to each instruction.**

_____ press 'Record' on the MD Player.   _____ put a disc in the MD Player.

_____ keep recording until the CD stops playing.   _____ adjust the volume.

_____ plug the cable into the 'phones' slot.   _____ close the cover on the MD Player.

B **Listen again and check your answers.**

4

A **Listen. Are these people sure about what they're saying? Circle *S* for *Sure* or *NS* for *Not Sure*.**

1. It's an MD player, isn't it?   S   NS

2. You have a computer, don't you?   S   NS

3. You put it in here, didn't you?   S   NS

4. You press this button, don't you?   S   NS

5. You turned it off, didn't you?   S   NS

B **Listen again and practice.**

How does it work?

5

A Listen and check (✔) the correct statement.

Listen for it

Right or *That's right* is another way of saying *That's correct.*

☐ The man learns how to look at the photos on his digital camera.

☐ The man learns how to download photos from his digital camera.

☐ The man learns how to take photos using his digital camera.

B Listen again and number the pictures (1–6).

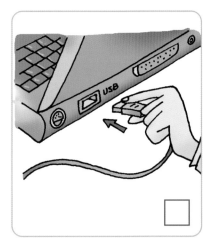

6

Listen and circle the answers that are right for you.

1. Yes, I do.	No, I don't.	**4.** Yes, I am.	No, I'm not.
2. Yes, I can.	No, I can't.	**5.** Yes, I have.	No, I haven't.
3. Yes, I have.	No, I haven't.	**6.** Yes, I do.	No, I don't.

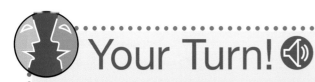

Your Turn! 🔊

Giving and understanding instructions

Sample Dialog

A: Can you tell me how to use this computer?

B: Sure. First you have to turn it on. Just press the 'Power' button.

A: OK. Do I have to open this now?

B: Yes. Open it, put in a disk, and then close it.

A: How do I open it? Do I press a button on the right side?

B: No, the button is on the front. You adjust the sound on the side.

Useful Expressions

- How do I turn it on?
- I don't know how to open it.
- What is this cable for?
- Move this switch to adjust the picture quality.
- You have to use the slot marked 'Cable In.'

Try this . . .

Choose an electronic item from the ones shown. Ask your partner how to use it. Repeat the instructions to your partner and then switch roles.

In Focus: *The mother of invention*

In a 1999 survey by the American Broadcasting Corporation (ABC), 30 percent of respondents chose the computer as the twentieth century's greatest invention, ahead of the car, electricity, television, and the telephone. *What do you think are some of the greatest inventions of the past 100 years? What are some inventions that you can't live without?*

I think rewriteable CDs are a great invention because you can store so much information.

I still think books are the best invention ever. We couldn't live without them.

The Internet is the world's greatest invention, because it has brought us all closer together.

Review

①

A Marcia is describing the type of home she's looking for. Listen and circle the correct information.

Skyline Real Estate			
Housing request form for: *Marcia Wheeler*			
Wants:	house	apartment	
No. of bedrooms:	1	2	3
Type:	furnished	semi-furnished	unfurnished
Furnishings:	bedroom	living room	dining room other: _____
Located close to:	university	downtown	subway bus routes
Monthly rent:	up to $_____		

B Listen again and check your answers.

②

A Listen to the conversations and number the pictures (1–4).

B Listen again and circle the things Alison can do.

1. **a.** type 60 words a minute
   b. type 70 words a minute
   c. type 75 words a minute

2. **a.** use the coffee machine
   b. use the phone system
   c. use the fax machine

3. **a.** speak French
   b. speak Spanish
   c. speak Chinese

4. **a.** use PictureShop software
   b. use AccountBook software
   c. use Exalt software

3

A Listen to the telephone recording. Number the correct places on the map (1–5).

1. Papa Romano's restaurant
2. Hollywood Cineplex
3. Sunnyvale Shopping Center
4. City Center subway station
5. Bus station

B Listen again and check your answers.

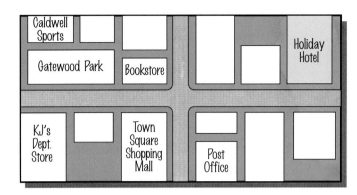

4

A Listen to the conversations. What department is each person looking for? Number the photos (1–5).

FURNITURE

TOYS

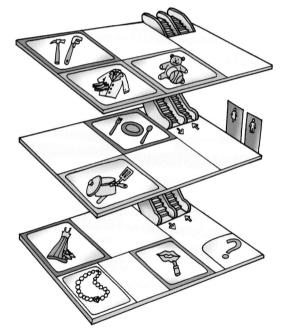

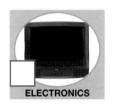

ELECTRONICS

SPORTS

LUGGAGE

B Listen again. Draw lines from the photos to the correct locations in the store.

5

Listen and circle the answers that are right for you.

1. No, it's quite close by.	It's not too far away.	It's quite far from here.
2. Yes, I do.	Not every day.	I never take it.
3. Yes, there are a lot.	There are a few.	No, there aren't.
4. I know a lot about them.	I know something about them.	I don't know anything about them.
5. Yes, I can.	I can try.	Sorry, I don't know how to use them.

UNIT 11

I usually get up at six.

Goals
- Identifying times and events
- Understanding schedules

1

A The pictures show the events in Nathan's daily routine. Correct the sentences below to match the pictures.

Nathan goes to the gym at eleven thirty. *(five thirty)*

He does his homework at six thirty.

He goes to bed at quarter after ten.

He plays pool with his friends at five thirty.

He watches TV with his friends at quarter to nine.

He eats dinner at ten to ten.

He gets to school at one thirty.

He has lunch at nine o'clock.

He gets up at twelve fifteen.

B **Brainstorm!** Work with a partner. Imagine at least three more events in Nathan's routine and the times they occur.

2

A Listen and number the times in the order you hear them (1–6).

☐

_____

☐

_____

☐

_____

☐

_____

☐

_____

☐

_____

B Listen again. Write the verb you hear under each clock.

3

A Listen to the questions and circle the best response.

1. Oh, about eight thirty.   About noon.

2. At five thirty.   Twelve thirty.

3. Around six thirty.   Oh, around two.

4. Ten forty-five.   Seven o'clock.

5. Around seven thirty.   Usually around eleven.

B Listen again and check your answers.

4

A Questions like *When do you usually get up?* are often reduced. Listen to the example.

> **Example:** When do you usually get up?   *When d'y usually get up?*

Listen to the sentences and circle *Reduced* or *Not Reduced*.

1. Reduced   Not reduced

2. Reduced   Not reduced

3. Reduced   Not reduced

4. Reduced   Not reduced

5. Reduced   Not reduced

6. Reduced   Not reduced

B Listen again and practice.

I usually get up at six.   **57**

5

A **Three people are describing their daily routines. Listen and fill in the blanks under _Event_.**

Listen for it

Well is used for emphasis or to pause before saying something.

Person	Event	Time
Linda	gets up	_____
	_____	6:00
	has lunch	_____
	_____	4:00
	gets home	_____
	_____	11:30
Stewart	leaves home	_____
	_____	9:00
	starts part-time job	_____
	_____	8:00
	watches TV	_____
	_____	11:30
Sophie	_____	7:00
	has lunch	_____
	_____	2:00
	meets with council	_____
	_____	6:00
	practices violin	_____

B **Listen again and fill in the blanks under _Time_.**

6

Listen and circle the answers that are right for you.

1. True   False   4. True   False

2. True   False   5. True   False

3. True   False   6. True   False

58   Unit 11

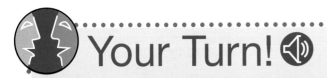# Your Turn! 🔊

Talking about your daily routine

Sample Dialog

A: What time do you get up in the morning?
B: I get up at about 7:00. Then I take a shower.
A: Do you have breakfast?
B: Yes. I eat and read the paper and then leave home at about 8:15.
A: Maybe you could get up earlier and study English from 7:00 to 7:30.
B: I like to sleep a little later than that, but I guess I could study.

Useful Expressions

- When do you usually have lunch?
- Usually at noon but sometimes a bit later.
- What do you do after school?
- I watch TV from 7:00 to 8:30 and then do my homework.
- Do you have any extra time in the morning?
- Could you study for an hour at lunch?

Try this . . . Ask about a partner's daily routine and write the times in the schedule below. Help your partner find some extra time to study English.

Daily Schedule

_____	Get up	_____	Get home
_____	Have breakfast	_____	Have dinner
_____	Go to school/work	_____	Watch TV/Do homework
_____	Have lunch	_____	Go to bed

In Focus: *A day in the life*

Hollywood stars are known for spending long days on the set while making movies. Tom Cruise once said a typical day for him begins at 4:30 a.m. and lasts as long as 18–20 hours. Famous musicians and celebrities in other fields have made similar statements. *Who are some of the most famous people in your country? What kinds of activities do you think make up their daily routines?*

Our prime minister must have a really busy schedule. He probably has to get up really early in the morning each day.

I think most actors in Hollywood probably have an easy working day. And they get paid a lot of money, too!

Anna Kournikova must have a tough daily schedule. She has to practice tennis—and also do lots of interviews with the media!

I'll have soup and a sandwich.

Goals
- Understanding food and drink orders
- Understanding and confirming reservations

1

A What is each person saying? Match the word balloons to the pictures.

1 What would you like to drink?

2 I'm sorry but we're fully booked on that date.

3 I'd like the steak, please.

4 Would you like to see the 7:00 or 9:30 show?

5 I'd like to order a pizza for delivery.

6 A table for five, please.

B Brainstorm! Work with a partner. Add at least three items to each page of the menu.

Main Dishes	Drinks	Desserts
Cheeseburger	Cola	Apple Pie
Steak	Coffee	Carrot Cake
_____	_____	_____
_____	_____	_____
_____	_____	_____

2

A Listen. Which of the food items is each person talking about? Check (✔) the correct item.

①  ☐  ☐

③ 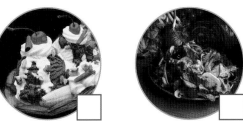 ☐ ☐

②  ☐  ☐

④  ☐  ☐

B Listen again and check your answers.

3

A Listen. Which people are making restaurant reservations? Circle *Yes* or *No*.

	Restaurant reservation?		Successful?		
Conversation 1	Yes	No	Yes	No	Unknown
Conversation 2	Yes	No	Yes	No	Unknown
Conversation 3	Yes	No	Yes	No	Unknown
Conversation 4	Yes	No	Yes	No	Unknown
Conversation 5	Yes	No	Yes	No	Unknown

B Listen again. Which people succeeded in making reservations? Circle *Yes*, *No*, or *Unknown*.

4

A Listen and check (✔) if *would/will* is reduced.

1. ____ Would you like to see the menu?

2. ____ Yes, I would like a menu.

3. ____ I would like a hamburger.

4. ____ What will you have to drink?

5. ____ Will that be all?

6. ____ I will have the sirloin.

B Listen again and practice.

5

A Listen. Are these people making reservations or ordering food? Circle *R* for *reservation* or *O* for *ordering food*.

1.
2.
3.
4.

R   O   R   O   R   O   R   O

B Listen again and check your answers.

6

A Listen. How many people are ordering? Circle the number.

1   2   3   4   5   6

Listen for it

Let's see is used when pausing to think or consider something.

B Listen again and check (✔) the orders.

7

A Listen and circle the best response.

1. Yes, I would.   A hamburger, please.   4. No, thank you.   Cream and sugar?

2. No, it doesn't.   Yes, you can.   5. Yes, I did.   Well done, please.

3. Small or large?   Sorry, we're fully booked.   6. Two tickets, please. At 2:30, please.

B Listen again and check your answers.

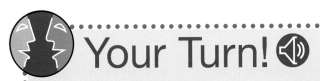

Your Turn! 🔊

Ordering food and taking orders

Sample Dialog

A: Are you ready to order?
B: Yes, I'll have the roast beef and a garden salad, please.
A: What kind of dressing would you like?
B: Thousand Island, please.
A: Anything to drink?
B: I'll have an iced tea.
A: OK. Coming right up.

Useful Expressions

- What would you like to order?
- How would you like that done?
- I'd like it medium rare, please.
- Did you say cola?
- Do you want milk and sugar with that?
- Would you like chocolate or red cherry?
- Would you like anything else?

menu

Soups
- Vegetable $3.50
- French Onion $3.95

Salads
- Garden Salad $2.95
- Caesar Salad $3.95

Main Dishes
- Sirloin Steak $9.95
- Roast Beef $11.95
- Deluxe Burger $6.95
  with cheese $7.50

Desserts
- Apple Pie $2.95
  with ice cream $3.50
- Cheesecake
  Cherry $3.95
  Chocolate $3.95

Drinks
- Cola/Juice/Milk
  small $1.95
  large $2.50
- Beer/Wine .... $3.95 per mug/glass
- Coffee/Tea $1.95

Try this . . .

Read the menu. Take turns being a restaurant server and a customer.

In Focus: *Mind your manners*

Most people learn proper table manners at an early age. But rules of etiquette in one country don't always apply to another. *What are some of the customs associated with eating in your country? What sorts of meal time behavior are unacceptable?*

In Japan, it's OK to make slurping sounds while eating noodles.

In Mexico, it's the custom to keep both hands above the table during a meal.

In France, it's the custom to eat salad after the main course.

UNIT 13

He shoots, he scores!

Goals
- Identifying sports
- Understanding sports broadcasts

1

A Match the words in the box with the correct sport. Some words may be used more than once.

game	serve	field	shoot	green	tackle	pass
court	match	putt	tournament	set	cup	score

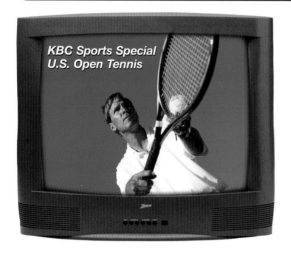

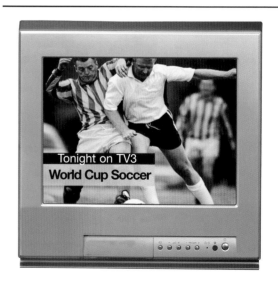

B **Brainstorm!** Work with a partner. Think of at least two other words that relate to each of the sports above.

2

 A Listen and circle the picture for each sport you hear.

B Listen again and check your answers.

3

Listen for it

Oh! is used to express surprise or to emphasize what you think about something.

 A Listen and answer *True* or *False*.

Commentary 1

1. The commentary is at a tennis match.	T	F	3. The weather is very hot.	T F
2. It is a match between two men.	T	F	4. One of the players is named Jim Stone.	T F

Commentary 2

1. The commentary is at a basketball game.	T	F	3. Chang scores.	T F
2. Chang and Wong are on the same team.	T	F	4. The game ends.	T F

Commentary 3

1. The commentary is at a golf tournament.	T	F	3. The ball is eight feet from the cup.	T F
2. Jenny Kim is Australian.	T	F	4. It is raining.	T F

B Listen again and check your answers.

4

 A Depending on the intonation, *Oh* can have many different meanings. Listen to the intonation of *Oh* and match each one with the correct ending.

1. Oh!   That's a real shame.

2. Oh?   That was a great shot.

3. Oh,   I see.

4. Oh.   I didn't know that.

5. Oh . . .   I haven't decided yet.

B Listen and check your answers. Then practice saying the sentences using the correct intonation.

5

A Listen to the soccer game report and complete the chart.

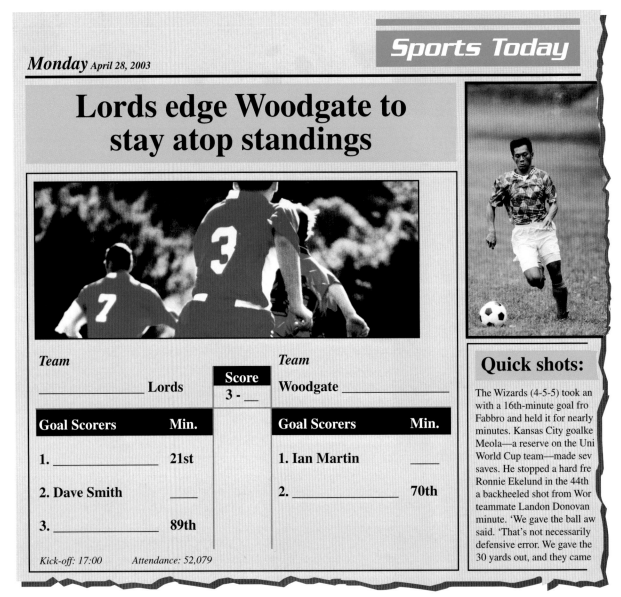

Sports Today

Monday *April 28, 2003*

Lords edge Woodgate to stay atop standings

Team		Score	Team	
_____ Lords		3 - __	Woodgate _____	

Goal Scorers	Min.		Goal Scorers	Min.
1. _____	21st		1. Ian Martin	____
2. Dave Smith	____		2. _____	70th
3. _____	89th			

Kick-off: 17:00   *Attendance: 52,079*

Quick shots:

The Wizards (4-5-5) took an with a 16th-minute goal fro Fabbro and held it for nearly minutes. Kansas City goalke Meola—a reserve on the Uni World Cup team—made sev saves. He stopped a hard fre Ronnie Ekelund in the 44th a backheeled shot from Wor teammate Landon Donovan minute. 'We gave the ball aw said. 'That's not necessarily defensive error. We gave the 30 yards out, and they came

B Listen again and check your answers.

6

Listen and circle the answers that are right for you.

1. Yes, I do.   No, I don't.
2. Yes, I am.   No, I'm not.
3. Yes, I do.   No, I don't.

4. Yes, I have.   No, I haven't.
5. Yes, I do.   No, I don't.
6. Yes, I am.   No, I'm not.

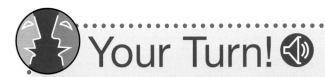

Your Turn! 🔊

Talking about sports

Sample Dialog

A: Do you watch a lot of sports on TV?
B: Not really. But I like to play golf.
A: I like golf, too. Are you a good golfer?
B: Yeah, pretty good. How about you?
A: I'm not very good at sports, but I watch a lot of sports on TV.
B: Oh, really? What kinds of sports do you watch?
A: Besides golf, I watch a lot of soccer and tennis matches.

Useful Expressions

- What's your favorite soccer team?
- Who's your favorite basketball player?
- How often do you go to baseball games?
- About once or twice a month.
- Do you ever listen to games on the radio?
- Do you play on any teams at school?

Try this . . .   Ask different classmates the questions below. When someone answers 'Yes,' write down the person's name. Ask follow-up questions to find out more information.

	Name	More information
Do you . . .		
1. watch a lot of sports on TV?	————	———————
2. read the sports news every day?	————	———————
3. play on a school/company sports team?	————	———————
4. listen to sports on the radio?	————	———————
5. like to go to professional sports events?	————	———————

In Focus: *National sports*

Golf is played in many countries around the world, but is considered the national sport in Scotland, where many people say it was invented at least 600 years ago. Similarly, baseball is called the 'national pastime' in the United States, and Australian Rules football was founded in Australia. *What is the national sport in your country? What do you know about its history? Can you explain some of the rules?*

> The English are crazy about football, or soccer. We started playing it here in 1863, and it's still the most popular sport in the country

> Everyone in Thailand learns *Muay Thai*, or kick-boxing. *Muay Thai* is 2,000 years old and is unlike any other martial art.

> Canada's national sport isn't ice hockey, it's lacrosse. Players try to score using a ball and sticks with nets on the end.

He shoots, he scores!

Do you want to see a movie?

G oals | • Recognizing invitations
• Identifying types of entertainment

1

A Match the picture with the phrase.

(1. have dinner) (3. go to a baseball game) (5. go dancing) (7. see a play)

(2. go to an art exhibition) (4. see a movie) (6. go to a concert)

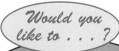
Would you like to . . . ?

B **Brainstorm!** Work with a partner. What are some other events to which you might invite someone? What other words or expressions might you use to invite that person?

2

A   Listen. Which are invitations? Circle *Y* for *Yes* or *N* for *No*.

1. Y N   2. Y N   3. Y N   4. Y N   5. Y N   6. Y N

B   Listen again and check your answers.

3

A   Listen to the announcement. How many different events do you hear? Circle the number.

4   5   6   7   8

B   Listen again and fill in the missing information.

Play: *The King's Revenge*
Place: _____
Time: _____

Basketball: *Knights vs. Towers*
Place: _____
Time: _____

Concert: *City Symphony Orchestra*
Place: _____
Time: _____

Event: *Video Dance Party*
Place: _____
Time: _____

4

A   Listen. Do the questions have rising (↗) or falling (↘) intonation? Circle the correct answer.

1. ↗ ↘   2. ↗ ↘   3. ↗ ↘   4. ↗ ↘   5. ↗ ↘   6. ↗ ↘

B   Listen again and practice.

Do you want to see a movie?

5

A Listen to the conversations. What types of entertainment are the people talking about? Number the sections of the entertainment guide (1–5).

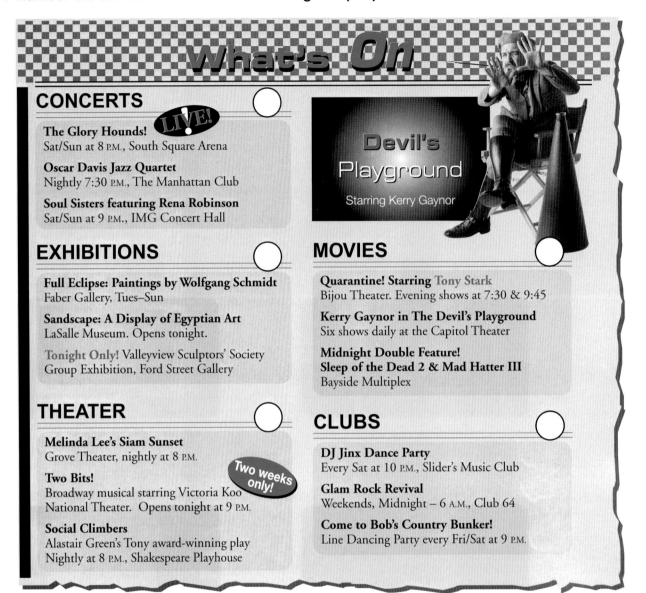

What's On

CONCERTS ⬤

The Glory Hounds! LIVE!
Sat/Sun at 8 P.M., South Square Arena

Oscar Davis Jazz Quartet
Nightly 7:30 P.M., The Manhattan Club

Soul Sisters featuring Rena Robinson
Sat/Sun at 9 P.M., IMG Concert Hall

Devil's Playground
Starring Kerry Gaynor

EXHIBITIONS ⬤

Full Eclipse: Paintings by Wolfgang Schmidt
Faber Gallery, Tues–Sun

Sandscape: A Display of Egyptian Art
LaSalle Museum. Opens tonight.

Tonight Only! Valleyview Sculptors' Society
Group Exhibition, Ford Street Gallery

MOVIES ⬤

Quarantine! Starring Tony Stark
Bijou Theater. Evening shows at 7:30 & 9:45

Kerry Gaynor in The Devil's Playground
Six shows daily at the Capitol Theater

Midnight Double Feature!
Sleep of the Dead 2 & Mad Hatter III
Bayside Multiplex

THEATER ⬤

Melinda Lee's Siam Sunset
Grove Theater, nightly at 8 P.M.

Two Bits!
Broadway musical starring Victoria Koo
National Theater. Opens tonight at 9 P.M.

Two weeks only!

Social Climbers
Alastair Green's Tony award-winning play
Nightly at 8 P.M., Shakespeare Playhouse

CLUBS ⬤

DJ Jinx Dance Party
Every Sat at 10 P.M., Slider's Music Club

Glam Rock Revival
Weekends, Midnight – 6 A.M., Club 64

Come to Bob's Country Bunker!
Line Dancing Party every Fri/Sat at 9 P.M.

B Listen again. For each conversation, circle the event the people plan to attend.

6

Listen and circle the answers that are right for you.

1. OK.   Sorry, I can't tonight.

2. Yes, I would.   No, I wouldn't.

3. Great, I'd love to go.   I'm afraid I can't make it.

4. All right.   Sorry, I'm not really interested.

5. Sounds great.   No, thanks.

Listen for it

Come on! is an informal way of expressing disbelief or encouraging someone to do something.

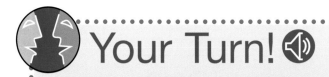

Your Turn! 🔊

Making and responding to invitations

Sample Dialog

A: Would you like to see the Soul Sisters on Saturday?
B: I'd like to, but I'm going to see 'Two Bits!' at the National Theater.
A: Oh, that's too bad. Well, how about going on Sunday?
B: Well, I'd rather see the exhibition at the Faber Gallery.
A: That sounds good. What's the exhibition called?
B: 'Full Eclipse: Paintings by Wolfgang Schmidt.'
A: All right. I'll see you at the gallery around 8:00.

Useful Expressions

- I have two tickets for the Glory Hounds concert. Want to go?
- I'd love to. What time does it start?
- Let's go to the Ford Street Gallery tonight.
- No, thanks. I'm not really interested.
- What are you doing on Tuesday night?
- Do you want to see a movie?
- Sorry, I can't make it that night. How about Thursday?

Try this . . . Choose five events in the *What's On* section in Task 5 and invite a different classmate to attend each one. Write the details in the calendar.

Weekly Planner

Monday	Tuesday	Wednesday	Thursday	Friday	Saturday	Sunday

In Focus: *Dating customs*

For generations in North America, it was considered inappropriate for women to invite men on dates. This custom began to change in the 1940s and '50s. Inspired by a popular comic strip character, many high schools and colleges inaugurated 'Sadie Hawkins Dances,' occasions when a woman was expected to attend with the man of her choice. *What are some of the past and present customs associated with dating in your country?*

In Japan, it's unusual for someone's parents to meet the person he or she is dating until they decide to get married.

It was once a custom in the United States for adult chaperons to accompany young couples on dates.

Young people in Spain often meet dates through *pandilla*, clubs or groups of friends with the same interests.

Do you want to see a movie? **71**

UNIT 15

What's the weather like?

Goals
- Identifying types of weather
- Understanding weather reports

1

A **What's the weather like in Europe? Match each weather report to one of the cities on the map. Draw lines to the correct cities.**

1 . . . rain across the city with the temperature at a very humid twenty-seven degrees . . .

2 . . . it's a warm and sunny eighteen degrees in the city this morning . . .

3 . . . snow will continue all day, and the temperature will stay at about minus five . . .

4 . . . right now, it's partly cloudy with the temperature a cool eight degrees . . .

5 . . . cloudy and cold this morning, with a temperature of about minus five degrees . . .

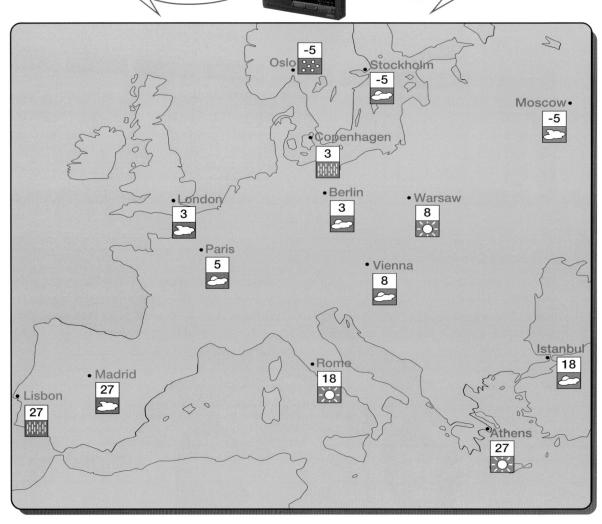

B **Brainstorm! Work with a partner. What's the weather like in your city on a typical day in July? What's it like in January, April, and October?**

72

2

A Listen. Is the report about news or weather? Check (✔) the correct column.

City	News	Weather	Key Words
Seoul	_____	_____	_____
Bangkok	_____	_____	_____
Taipei	_____	_____	_____
Osaka	_____	_____	_____
Kuala Lumpur	_____	_____	_____
Jakarta	_____	_____	_____

B Listen again. Write the key words that helped you decide.

3

A Listen and circle the picture that matches each conversation.

1.

2.

3.

B Listen again and check your answers.

4

A Listen. Which is more important, the weather or the time? Circle *W* for *Weather* or *T* for *Time*.

Listen for it

That's right! is used when you remember something or are reminded of it.

Ex: It will be **warm** tomorrow.   **T**   It will be warm **tomorrow**. **W**

1. W   T   2. W   T   3. W   T   4. W   T   5. W   T   6. W   T

B Listen again and check your answers.

5

A
Listen to the weather forecasts and write the temperature for each city.

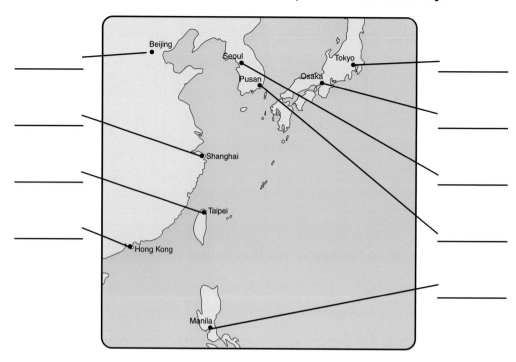

Beijing

Seoul

Tokyo

Pusan Osaka

Shanghai

Taipei

Hong Kong

Manila

B
Listen again. Where might you need these things? Write the name of a city under each item.

1. _____

2. _____

3. _____

4. _____

5. _____

6. _____

6

Listen and circle the answers that are right for you.

| 1. Yes, I do. | No, I don't. | 3. Yes, it was. | No, it wasn't. | 5. Yes, I do. | No, I don't. |
| 2. Yes, it is. | No, it isn't. | 4. Yes, I am. | No, I'm not. | 6. Yes, I did. | No, I didn't. |

Your Turn! 🔊

Talking about the weather

Sample Dialog

A: Hello, Alison? It's Geoff. I'm calling from Boracay.
B: Geoff! Hi! How's your vacation going?
A: Great! The Philippines is beautiful!
B: How's the weather? I'll bet it's really nice.
A: Yeah, sunny and very hot. I think it's about 33 degrees.
B: Wow, that is hot! What did you do today?
A: We went surfing this morning and scuba diving after lunch.

Useful Expressions

- It's cold and snowy.
- What's the temperature?
- I think it's about 10 below.
- What's the weather forecast for tomorrow?
- It's supposed to be warm and sunny.
- It's great weather for skiing.
- The weather is ideal for sunbathing.

Try this . . .

Imagine you are on vacation in one of the cities on the map in Task 5. Write down what the weather is like and two or three things that you did today. Tell a partner. Ask about your partner's vacation.

In Focus: *Winter of our discontent*

Once known simply as the 'winter blues,' Seasonal Affected Disorder (SAD) is now recognized by doctors as a type of depression. The shortage of daylight during the winter months is believed to cause a chemical imbalance in the brain. Symptoms of the illness, which include sleep problems, headaches, anxiety, and mood changes, are often treated with light therapy. *In what ways does the weather affect your mood?*

Hot weather makes me feel really tired. I just don't want to do anything.

I am always really happy when it rains. I never feel depressed at all.

I love when it snows. It makes me feel happy and romantic.

Review

Units 11–15

1

A Listen to the conversations and number the posters (1–4).

New York Knights vs Western U. Warriors

Killdeer Park
Sunday July 23,
2:00 P.M.

Accept   Decline

LIVE IN CONCERT
Eddie Wilson

Bridgeport Hall
Sat. July 15, 8 P.M.

Accept   Decline

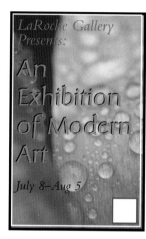

LaRoche Gallery
Presents:
An Exhibition of Modern Art

July 8–Aug 5

Accept   Decline

Winston's has arrived!

Grand Opening:
Friday, July 28,
7:30 P.M.

Accept   Decline

B Does the person accept or decline the invitation? Listen again and circle *Accept* or *Decline*.

2

A Listen and write Jenny's order.

Surf 'n' Turf

1 chef's salad

B Listen again and check your answers.

3

A Soccer star Karl Kessel is describing his daily routine. Listen and match the times to the activities.

(has breakfast)   (gets up)   (watches game tapes)   (does warm-up exercises)

(8:30) (9:20) (10:00) (11:00) (12:30) (2:00) (4:45) (5:30)

(gets to stadium)   (eats lunch)   (plays soccer)   (has team meeting)

B Listen again and check your answers.

4

A Listen to the sports broadcasts and fill in the results.

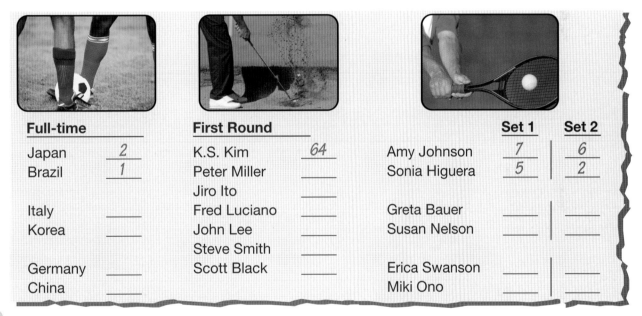

Full-time		First Round			Set 1	Set 2
Japan	2	K.S. Kim	64	Amy Johnson	7	6
Brazil	1	Peter Miller	___	Sonia Higuera	5	2
		Jiro Ito	___			
Italy	___	Fred Luciano	___	Greta Bauer	___	___
Korea	___	John Lee	___	Susan Nelson	___	___
		Steve Smith	___			
Germany	___	Scott Black	___	Erica Swanson	___	___
China	___			Miki Ono	___	___

B Listen again and check your answers.

5

Listen and circle the answers that are right for you.

1. Usually by 11.   Between 11 and 12.   Sometime after 12.

2. No, I don't.   Yes, sugar, too.   Yes, I do.

3. Hardly ever.   Sometimes.   Yes, quite a lot.

4. No, thanks.   Let me check my schedule.   Sounds great.

5. Terrible.   Not bad.   Great.

UNIT **16**

How did you meet your wife?

G oals
- Identifying people through description
- Understanding a personal narrative

1

A What qualities do you look for in your ideal date? Use the scale to rate how important each item is to you. Then share your answers with a partner.

Ideal Date Questionnaire

		Not important → Very important						
Appearance	Face (good-looking, cute)	0	1	2	3	4	5
	Body (attractive, athletic)	0	1	2	3	4	5
	Hair (length, color)	0	1	2	3	4	5
	Height	0	1	2	3	4	5
Background/Employment	Level of education	0	1	2	3	4	5
	Secure job/finances	0	1	2	3	4	5
Personality/Interests	Sense of humor	0	1	2	3	4	5
	Likes to talk/outgoing	0	1	2	3	4	5
	Similar interests/hobbies	0	1	2	3	4	5
Other	Age	0	1	2	3	4	5
	Same religion/beliefs	0	1	2	3	4	5
	Same cultural background	0	1	2	3	4	5
	_____	0	1	2	3	4	5
	_____	0	1	2	3	4	5

B Where do people meet new friends? Write numbers in the boxes.

> 1 = This is a common way to meet people.
> 2 = This is kind of unusual.
> 3 = This is very unusual.

☐ at school ☐ at work ☐ at a shopping mall

☐ through a dating agency ☐ through a friend or relative ☐ at a party

☐ at a health club ☐ at a nightclub ☐ through the Internet

C **Brainstorm!** Work with a partner. List at least three adjectives to describe your appearance and personality. Share your list with a partner. Does your partner agree?

2

A Three people are describing how they met their husband or wife. Listen and fill in the husband or wife's name.

Person	Name	How they met
Chuck		
Liz		
Charlotte		

B Listen again and write down how each couple met.

3

A Listen to the conversation and number the information (1–7) in the order you hear it.

☐ What he likes   ☐ Eye color

☐ Height   ☐ What he does

☐ Name   ☐ Hair color

☐ Where he works

B Listen again. What are the three things Anthony likes?

1. _____

2. _____

3. _____

> **Listen for it**
>
> *Kind of* is another way of saying *a little bit* or *somewhat*.

4

A In spoken English, *kind of* and *sort of* are sometimes reduced to *kinda* and *sorta*. Listen to the examples. Then listen and circle *Reduced* or *Not Reduced*.

> **Ex. 1:** I'm *kind of* tired. I'm *kinda* tired.   **Ex. 2:** She's *sort of* tall. She's *sorta* tall.

1. Reduced	Not Reduced	4. Reduced	Not Reduced
2. Reduced	Not Reduced	5. Reduced	Not Reduced
3. Reduced	Not Reduced	6. Reduced	Not Reduced

B Listen again and practice.

How did you meet your wife?

5

A
Listen to the people describe themselves on an introduction agency tape. Check (✔) the information that is true for each person.

	Ellen	John	Shelley	Henry	Paul	Aida
Works at home	_____	_____	_____	_____	_____	_____
Kind of short	_____	_____	_____	_____	_____	_____
Wants a tennis partner	_____	_____	_____	_____	_____	_____
Likes to travel	_____	_____	_____	_____	_____	_____
Works in a school	_____	_____	_____	_____	_____	_____
Likes to have fun	_____	_____	_____	_____	_____	_____
Likes to talk	_____	_____	_____	_____	_____	_____
Plans to be a doctor	_____	_____	_____	_____	_____	_____

B
Listen again and find each person. Label each picture with the correct name. Who would make the best partners?

_____

_____

_____

_____

_____

_____

6

Listen and circle the answers that are right for you.

1. Yes, I am.   I guess I'm kind of average.   Not really.

2. Oh, all the time.   Now and then.   Hardly ever.

3. Blue.   Brown.   Gray.

4. Yes, I love them.   I don't mind them.   No, I don't.

5. Doesn't everyone?   Occasionally.   No, I prefer a quiet time.

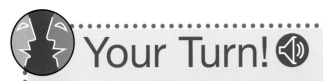

Your Turn! 🔊

Describing yourself

Sample Dialog

A: Could you tell me a little bit about yourself?
B: Well, I'm 31. I'm kind of tall. I have brown hair and green eyes.
A: And how would you describe your personality?
B: I guess I'm kind of an outgoing guy.
A: OK. What kind of person would you like to meet?
B: I'm looking for someone who's also tall, who likes to talk and have fun.
A: I just need to find out a few more things . . .

Useful Expressions

- Could you describe your appearance for me?
- I'm about average height and I have blonde hair.
- I'd like to meet someone who shares my interests.
- What sorts of things do you do in your spare time?
- Does your partner have to be the same age as you?
- I want to meet someone with a good sense of humor.

Try this . . .

Imagine you work for an introduction agency. Your partner phones you and wants to meet someone. Find out about your partner and the kind of person he or she wants to meet. Take notes. Then, switch roles.

Description of client:
_____
_____
_____

Client wants to meet someone who:
_____
_____
_____

In Focus: *Love at first sight*

Advice columnist Jeanne Phillips and her daughter Pauline, who answer letters in the popular 'Dear Abby' column, occasionally run readers' accounts of how they met their spouses. According to the letters, people have met future partners in places ranging from train cars to World War II bomb shelters. *Do you have a story about how you met your partner or a close friend? Do you know any couples or friends who met under unusual circumstances?*

I met my best friend on the subway. We got off at the same stop and have hardly been apart since.

My girlfriend and I grew up together. I guess we'll probably get married some day.

My best friend met her husband on a TV show called 'Blind Date.'

How did you meet your wife? 81

UNIT

Why don't we buy a new car?

Goals | • Recognizing suggestions
• Understanding objections

1

A One person in each picture is making a suggestion. Match each person with the correct suggestion.

1 Why don't we buy this one?

2 I think we should go to this place.

3 How about having it on June 3rd?

4 Let's try it!

B What could the other person say to accept each suggestion? And to reject it? Number the sentences in each column (1–4).

Accept
_____ OK. That sounds like a good date.
_____ Yeah, it looks like the perfect size.
_____ All right. I've never tried it.
_____ Great! Seems like there's lots to do there.

Reject
_____ I don't think so. It's too hot then.
_____ I'd prefer somewhere else. It's too far away.
_____ No, that one is too small.
_____ I'd rather not. It looks dangerous!

C **Brainstorm!** How else could the person accept or reject the suggestion. Make a list with a partner.

2

A

Listen. Is the person making a suggestion, accepting a suggestion, or rejecting a suggestion? Circle *Suggest*, *Accept*, or *Reject*.

1. Suggest   Accept   Reject   4. Suggest   Accept   Reject

2. Suggest   Accept   Reject   5. Suggest   Accept   Reject

3. Suggest   Accept   Reject   6. Suggest   Accept   Reject

B

Listen again and check your answers.

3

A

Listen to the conversations and check (✔) *True* or *False*.

1. Damon suggests fixing the washer. ☐ True ☐ False

2. Sherry accepts Hiroko's suggestion. ☐ True ☐ False

3. Sherry accepts Jack's suggestion to play golf. ☐ True ☐ False

4. Sherry and Isabel are going to an art exhibition on Sunday. ☐ True ☐ False

5. Jeff and Sherry are having dinner together on Saturday. ☐ True ☐ False

B

Listen again. Circle the names of the people who are having dinner together on Saturday.

Anne	Damon	Hiroko	Isabel
Jack	Jeff	Sherry	

Listen for it

That's fine is used to agree to something.

4

A

In spoken English, people sometimes drop unneeded words. Listen to the example.

Ex: I have some bad news, Damon.   ~~I have some~~ bad news, Damon.

Listen and draw a line through the words that are dropped.

1. It looks kind of old.

2. Do you know where it is?

3. Let's do it another time, then.

4. Are you home already?

5. Do you mind if I come?

6. I'm sorry I'm late.

B

Listen again and practice.

Why don't we buy a new car?

5

A **Paul and Emi are deciding on a movie to rent. Listen and circle the objections you hear.**

Listen for it

No way! is an informal way of expressing strong disagreement.

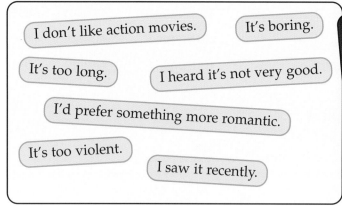

I don't like action movies.   It's boring.

It's too long.   I heard it's not very good.

I'd prefer something more romantic.

It's too violent.

I saw it recently.

B **Listen again and check your answers. Which movie do they decide to rent?**

_____

6

A **Listen to Tom and Sally planning their vacation. How many suggestions does Sally make? Circle the number.**

2   3   4   5   6   7

B **Listen again and fill in the blanks.**

Suggestion	Objection
fly to _____ for a couple of weeks ⟶	travel packages too expensive
postpone vacation until spring ⟶	too busy at _____
go _____ at Sky Valley Resort ⟶	went there last year
go to New Year's Eve party in NYC ⟶	don't like _____

7

Imagine that a friend is making suggestions. Listen and circle the answers that are right for you.

1. You're right.   I think it's OK to speak our native language, too.

2. Great!   I don't think that's such a good idea.

3. That's a good idea.   Sorry, I'm busy tonight.

4. All right.   Thanks, but I have other plans.

5. Sounds great!   I'd rather go somewhere else.

Your Turn!

Making, accepting, and rejecting suggestions

Sample Dialog

A: Hey, why don't we go to a soccer game on Sunday?
B: I'd rather not. I'm not really interested in soccer.
A: Well, how about going shopping instead?
B: That sounds good. And let's have lunch at that new Italian place.
A: I'd prefer somewhere else. I had Italian food last night.
B: OK. Then how about trying the Vietnamese restaurant on Stanley Street?
A: All right. I've never had Vietnamese food.

Useful Expressions

- Do you have any suggestions?
- I think we should do something different.
- How do you feel about that?
- I'm not so sure about that.
- Can I make a suggestion?
- Sure, go ahead.
- That's a great idea!
- No, I'd rather not.

Try this . . .

List some activities you would like to do this weekend. Suggest them to your partner. Your partner will either accept or reject each one. Write down your partner's response. Then, switch roles.

Weekend ideas : *Partner's response*

In Focus: *Any suggestions?*

It may not be a high-tech device, but the suggestion box has probably done more to boost corporate efficiency over the years than even the most powerful computer. Suggestion boxes allow workers to recommend ways of making their jobs easier and offer employers the chance to save money—or make even more. *What suggestions do you have to make your English class, your school/company, your city, or your country run more efficiently?*

To make the country more efficient, let's reduce the number of politicians.

Let's improve the transit system by having more trains and buses.

How about if everyone tries to arrive on time for English class?

Why don't we buy a new car?

Goals
- Identifying personal qualities
- Understanding survey questions

1

A Look at the pictures. Use a word from the box to label each person.

1. creative	3. hardworking	5. talkative	7. fun-loving
2. impatient	4. disorganized	6. shy	8. stubborn

_____ _____ _____ _____

_____ _____ _____ _____

B Match each word from the box above with the one with the opposite meaning.

_____ patient   _____ outgoing   _____ unimaginative   _____ organized

_____ serious   _____ flexible   _____ quiet   _____ lazy

C Brainstorm! Work with a partner. List at least three important qualities for each of the following people: 1. English teacher, 2. best friend, 3. co-worker, 4. boss.

2

 A Listen and match the people to the words that describe them.

Jeffrey   Rae   Gloria   Keith   Irene   Phil

(patient)   (stubborn)   (quiet)   (disorganized)

(talkative)   (fun-loving)   (shy)   (lazy)

B Listen again and check your answers.

3

 A Three people are talking about the Chinese zodiac. Listen to the conversation and complete the chart.

Birth year	Creature	Characteristic
1972/1984	Rat	_____
1973/1985	Ox	Patient
1974/1986	Tiger	Smart
1975/1987	Rabbit	Easygoing
1976/1988	Dragon	Energetic
1977/1989	Snake	_____

Birth year	Creature	Characteristic
1966/1978	Horse	_____
1967/1979	Sheep	_____
1968/1980	Monkey	_____
1969/1981	Rooster	Reliable
1970/1982	Dog	Loyal
1971/1983	Pig	Generous

B Listen again. What animal was each of the three speakers born under?

Ben: _____   Taro: _____   Wendy: _____

4

 A Listen and check (✔) the word you hear first in each conversation.

Ex. ✔ quite ____ quiet   **2.** ____ brought ____ bought   **4.** ____ sick ____ six

1. ____ live ____ leave   **3.** ____ guess ____ guest   **5.** ____ right ____ light

B Listen again and practice.

She's kind of shy.   **87**

5

A Cindy is answering a magazine survey with her boyfriend Kevin. Read the survey. Then listen and circle Kevin's answers.

Listen for it

Go ahead is used to tell someone it's OK to continue.

Personality Survey

1. Do you think of yourself as:

    (a) lazy?

    (b) hardworking?

2. Are you more frequently:

    (a) impatient?

    (b) patient?

3. Would you say you are:

    (a) fun-loving?

    (b) serious?

4. With people, do you tend to be:

    (a) stubborn?

    (b) flexible?

5. Do you tend to be:

    (a) talkative?

    (b) quiet?

6. In most situations, are you:

    (a) shy?

    (b) outgoing?

7. Would you describe yourself as:

    (a) organized?

    (b) disorganized?

8. Do you consider yourself:

    (a) creative?

    (b) unimaginative?

B Listen again. Does Cindy agree with Kevin's answers? Circle *A* for *Agree* or *D* for *Disagree*.

1. A D	**3.** A D	**5.** A D	**7.** A D
2. A D	**4.** A D	**6.** A D	**8.** A D

6

Listen and circle the answers that are right for you.

1. Yes, I'd say so.	Sometimes.	Almost never.
2. Definitely.	Sort of.	Not especially.
3. Yes, I do.	Kind of.	Not really.
4. Yes, I would.	I wouldn't mind.	Definitely not.
5. Most of them are.	Some of them are.	None of them are.

Your Turn! 🔊

Asking and talking about personality traits

Sample Dialog

A: Do you think you're hardworking or lazy?
B: I guess I'm lazy. I really don't like to work hard.
A: So, would you say you're a fun-loving person?
B: Yes. I'm definitely not a very serious person.
A: Why do you think so?
B: Well, I love to go to parties and have a good time.
A: OK. Do you tend to be a stubborn person . . . ?

Useful Expressions

- How would you describe yourself?
- I'm a hardworking person but fun-loving, too.
- I'm pretty shy. I don't really like to meet new people.
- What's your new boyfriend like?
- Would you say you're a talkative person?

Try this . . .

Work with a partner. Role-play the conversation in Task 5 and complete the survey with your partner's information. Give reasons for your answers. Switch roles.

Personality Survey

1. (a) lazy
   (b) hardworking

2. (a) impatient
   (b) patient

3. (a) fun-loving
   (b) serious

4. (a) stubborn
   (b) flexible

5. (a) talkative
   (b) quiet

6. (a) shy
   (b) outgoing

7. (a) organized
   (b) disorganized

8. (a) creative
   (b) unimaginative

In Focus: *Chinese zodiac*

The Chinese zodiac—the rotating cycle of twelve animal signs—was a folk method for naming the years in ancient China. According to tradition, all people born under the same sign are said to possess a fixed set of character traits. Find your animal sign in the chart in Task 3. *How do you feel about the character traits associated with each sign? Are they accurate descriptions? Do you believe in the Chinese zodiac?*

I was born in the Year of the Rat but I'm lazy, not hardworking.

I'm a Snake but I'm not very serious at all. I'm more of a fun-loving person.

I'm reliable like most Roosters. I'm also talkative and kind of creative.

Are you free on Tuesday?

Goals
- Understanding schedules
- Identifying and confirming appointments

1

A Look at the pictures showing events in Suzanne's schedule. Use the times and dates under the pictures and the words in the box to fill in Suzanne's planner.

aerobics class	dentist's appointment	debating team meeting
volunteer work	play rehearsal	part-time job
music practice	hair salon appointment	

Wed. 5:30–8 p.m.

Tue. 4:30 p.m.

Wed. noon–1 p.m.

Tue. 7:30–9 p.m.

Tue. 10 a.m.

Wed. 3:30 p.m.

Tue. 1:15 p.m.

Wed. 9:30 a.m.

Tuesday, June 5

9 a.m.

11 a.m.

1 p.m.

3 p.m.

5 p.m.

7 p.m.

9 p.m.

Wednesday, June 6

9 a.m.

11 a.m.

1 p.m.

3 p.m.

5 p.m.   *5:30 part-time job*

7 p.m.   ↓

        8:00

9 p.m.

B Make a list of your own appointments for this week. Tell your partner.

A Listen. What appointments do the people have?
Number the photos (1–5).

Listen for it

Actually means *in fact* or *to be honest*.

Day: _____

Time: _____

Day: _____

Time: _____

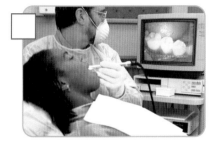

Day: _____

Time: _____

Day: _____

Time: _____

Day: _____

Time: _____

B Listen again and write the correct day and time under each photo.

A Alicia is talking to her mother on the phone. Listen and complete her calendar.

17 FRIDAY	18 SATURDAY	19 SUNDAY
4:30 p.m. hair salon appointment	11 a.m.	9:30 p.m.
6 p.m.	1 - 5:30 p.m.	noon - 5 p.m. volunteer work
7:30 p.m. date with Ken	6 - 10:00 p.m.	7 p.m.

B Listen again and check your answers.
When is Alicia planning to visit her family? _____

Are you free on Tuesday? 91

4

A Listen to the examples. Notice how the highlighted sounds are pronounced.

> **Ex. 1:** I saw John the other day.   **Ex. 2:** I saw John on the deck.

Now listen and put the words in the correct column.

> May   station   friend   letter   eight   neighbor   met   center   kept   mail

/eɪ/	/e/
day	*deck*

B Listen again and practice.

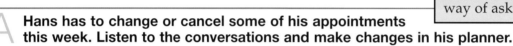

Listen for it

How come? is an informal way of asking *Why?*

5

A Hans has to change or cancel some of his appointments this week. Listen to the conversations and make changes in his planner.

7 Mon.	~~Noon–Lunch with Kerry~~ _____ 4–6 p.m. band practice	**10** Thu.	Staff meeting @ 4:30 p.m. _____ 7:30 p.m. date with Alison
8 Tue.	11:00 a.m.—Doctor's appointment Noon—Lunch with Kerry 6:30–10 p.m. Play rehearsal	**11** Fri.	8 a.m.—Golf with Aaron 1–4 p.m. volunteer at school _____
9 Wed.	Art class—4:00 p.m. _____ Band concert @ 8:00 p.m.	**12** Sat.	Football team party 9 p.m.
		13 Sun.	7:30 p.m. dinner with Mom & Dad _____

B Listen again and check your answers.

6

Listen and circle the answers that are right for you.

1. Before 6:00.   Between 6:00 and 7:00.   After 7:00.

2. No, not really.   I have some work to finish.   Yes, I'm busy tonight.

3. Pretty full.   I have some free time.   Wide open.

4. I don't really have time.   I'll have to check.   Shouldn't be a problem.

5. Any night is OK.   Friday or Saturday.   I'll check my schedule.

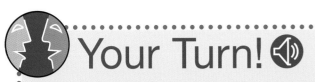

Your Turn! 🔊

Making and changing appointments

Sample Dialog

A: Hey, are we still doing that charity fun run on Saturday?

B: Yeah. Oh, but there's a change in the time for the basketball team party on Friday. It's now at 8:00.

A: Really? I'd better write that down.

B: Oh, and I forgot to tell you that basketball practice is canceled this week.

A: So, there's no practice on Tuesday at 4:30?

B: That's right.

Useful Expressions

- What are we doing on Saturday at 7:30?
- We're already doing something at that time.
- We have a study group meeting on Wednesday at 3:00.
- What time are we playing tennis?
- Basketball practice starts at 4:30.
- How about changing the time to 5:00?

Try this . . .

Imagine you and your partner are college roommates. The planner shows the activities you're planning to do together this week. Change or cancel some of your plans and tell your partner. Then, switch roles.

Weekly Planner

Mon.	study group meeting 3:00 P.M.
Tue.	basketball practice 4:30 P.M.
Wed.	tennis game 8:30 A.M.
Thu.	2:00 P.M. volunteer work @ Student Center
Fri.	basketball team party 9:00 P.M.
Sat.	charity fun run @ 7:00 A.M.
Sun.	

In Focus: *Better late than never*

In North America and many other parts of the world, it is not usually necessary to be on time for casual social gatherings. When invited to a dinner party, for example, people generally arrive 'casually late,' which means about a half-hour later than the appointed time. On the other hand, punctuality is considered essential when it comes to formal gatherings like weddings. *What's the attitude toward punctuality in your country? Are there any situations in which it is OK to arrive late? What about arriving early?*

Most people I know think punctuality is important but being late is not so bad.

Being late for a business meeting is unacceptable but for social events it's OK.

It's perfectly fine to arrive late for an appointment. People actually expect it.

How do you like to learn?

Goals
- Identifying learning styles
- Understanding information in a lecture

1

A **What are the students doing? Use the words in the box to label each picture.**

taking notes	listening to a tape	reading a textbook
attending a lecture	asking questions	using a computer
studying in a library	taking part in a discussion	doing an experiment

The students are learning by . . .

1. _____

2. _____

3. _____

4. _____

5. _____

6. _____

7. _____

8. _____

9. _____

B **Brainstorm! Which of the above activities helps you learn the best? Can you think of any other methods that help you learn? Make a list with a partner.**

2

A
Listen to the lecture on learning styles and complete each sentence.

Auditory learners learn best by _____

Visual learners learn best by _____

Tactile/Kinesthetic learners learn best by _____

B
Listen again and check your answers.

3

A
Listen to people describing their study habits. For each person, decide which type of learner they are. Circle *Auditory*, *Visual*, or *Tactile/Kinesthetic*.

1. Auditory	Visual	Tactile/Kinesthetic	**4.** Auditory	Visual	Tactile/Kinesthetic
2. Auditory	Visual	Tactile/Kinesthetic	**5.** Auditory	Visual	Tactile/Kinesthetic
3. Auditory	Visual	Tactile/Kinesthetic	**6.** Auditory	Visual	Tactile/Kinesthetic

B
Listen again. Do any of the people belong in more than one category?

4

A
Anna is answering questions to find out what her learning style is. Listen and number the questions (1–6) in the order you hear them.

Listen for it

So? is an informal way of saying *What happened next?* or *What's the conclusion?*

Questions	Answers
____ How do you learn how a computer works?	_____
____ What's the last book you read for fun?	_____
____ What do you do when you're not sure how to spell a word?	_____
____ How do you study for a test?	_____
____ What do you think of when you hear the word C-A-T?	_____
____ What kind of class did you like best?	_____

B
Listen again and write Anna's answers in the spaces. What kind of learner is Anna?

Auditory

Visual

Tactile/Kinesthetic

How do you like to learn?

A Listen and circle the right answer for you.

1. a. Read the instruction manual.
   b. Ask someone to explain it to me.
   c. Figure it out for myself, without using the manual.

2. a. A comic book.
   b. A novel.
   c. A quiz book.

3. a. Write it down and see if it looks right.
   b. Sound it out.
   c. Use a dictionary.

4. a. Read my notes to myself several times.
   b. Read my notes out loud several times.
   c. Rewrite my notes several times.

5. a. Slide presentation.
   b. Lecture.
   c. Demonstration.

6. a. Art class.
   b. Music class.
   c. Physical education/gym class.

7. a. By e-mail.
   b. By phone.
   c. In a meeting.

B Listen again and check your answers. What kind of learner are you?

> **Scoring:** More (a) answers suggests you are a **visual learner.**
> More (b) answers suggests you are an **auditory learner.**
> More (c) answers suggests you are a **tactile/kinesthetic learner.**

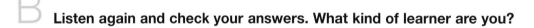

A Listen to the stressed syllables in the example.

> **Ex.:** You <u>learn</u> to <u>speak</u> by <u>speak</u>ing.

B Listen and underline the stressed syllables in each sentence.

1. They learned to read by reading.

2. I like to learn by touching.

3. I used to learn Chinese.

4. She studied Japanese in school.

5. I read the book in English.

6. I prefer to work on my own.

Check your answers with a partner. Which sentences have the same stress pattern as the example?

C Listen again and practice.

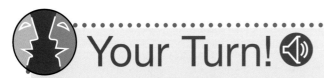

Your Turn! 🔊

Asking and talking about learning styles

Sample Dialog

A: Do you tend to learn a lot in lectures?
B: Not really. I usually can't remember much from lectures.
A: What if the lecturer draws diagrams on the board?
B: Yeah, that makes it easier. I also learn more when I draw my own diagrams.
A: Do you like to study from textbooks?
B: Sometimes. It helps if the textbook has a lot of illustrations.
A: Sounds like you're a visual learner.

Useful Expressions

- Do you prefer to read a textbook or listen to a lecture?
- I learn a lot more when I listen to a lecture.
- Are you better at using a map or listening to directions?
- I'm better at using a map. I can't remember directions.
- What's the easiest way for you to learn something?
- Do you think role-plays help you to learn?

Try this . . .

Interview your partner about his/her learning experiences and preferences. Use the words below to help you. Write down your partner's responses.

- Lectures • Demonstrations
- Map-reading • Textbooks
- Studying for tests
- Class projects
- Graphs and diagrams

In Focus: *Teaching styles*

As with learning, there are a number of different styles or methods of teaching ranging from lecturing and conducting demonstrations to leading discussions, setting tasks, and posing problems. *What are the most common teaching methods used in your country? Are any changes needed in the way students are taught?*

Lecturing is the most common method, but discussions are more useful.

The best way to teach is by having students solve actual problems.

Teachers who use case studies give their students real-world experience.

Review

Units 16–20

1

 A Listen to Andy, Craig, Mel, and Stephen describe themselves on a dating agency tape. Write the correct name under each photo.

_____ _____ _____ _____

(skiing)   (swimming)   (travel)   (concerts)   (reading)

(dancing)   (tennis)   (parties)   (movies)   (volunteering)

B Listen again and draw lines from the people to the activities they like. One activity is extra.

2

A Listen as Linda describes each of the men above. Match the names to the personality traits. Write *A* for *Andy*, *C* for *Craig*, *M* for *Mel*, and *S* for *Stephen*.

_____ fun-loving   _____ talkative   _____ shy   _____ outgoing

_____ quiet   _____ impatient   _____ hardworking   _____ serious

B Listen again and circle the personality traits she likes. Cross out the ones she dislikes.

3

A Listen to the conversations. Check (✔) the two suggestions you hear in each conversation.

1. see a movie ( )   **2.** eat dinner ( )   **3.** buy a car ( )   **4.** play tennis ( )

rent a video ( )   make lunch ( )   sell the car ( )   watch tennis ( )

go to the drive-in ( )   have a snack ( )   wash the car ( )   teach tennis ( )

B Listen again. Which suggestions are accepted? Underline them.

4

A Listen and check (✔) the times you hear.

B Listen again and match the times with the correct pictures.

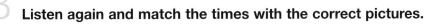

5

Listen and circle the answers that are right for you.

1. Yes, every day.   Sometimes I do.   No, I never wear them.

2. Yes, I think so.   It depends on the situation.   No, not at all.

3. I'm free all day.   I'm not sure.   I'm really busy.

4. Listening to music.   Going to movies.   Reading books.

5. I'm a lot more confident. I'm a bit more confident.   I'm about the same.

Language Summaries

Unit 1

Offering greetings
- Hello. / Hi.
- How's everything? / How's it going? / How are things?
  Not bad. / Pretty good, thanks.
- Hi. How are you?
  Fine, thanks. And you?

Introducing yourself
- Hello, I'm Dan. What's your name?
  My name's Francisco. Nice to meet you, Dan.
- Hi, I'm John. Pleased to meet you.
  Pleased to meet you, too. I'm Sam.
- How do you do? My name's Bill Jones.
  Nice to meet you, Bill. I'm Jerry Reynolds.
- Hi. I don't think we've met. I'm Li-wen Chu.
  Good to meet you, Li-wen. I'm Ann Rivers.

Starting an informal conversation
- Hello, you must be a friend of John's.
  Yes, that's right. I'm Joe's.
  No, actually I'm a friend of Amy's.
- Excuse me. Are you Jill Davis?
  Yes, I am.
  No, I'm Amanda Bell.
- Hi, are you enjoying the party? / So, are you having a good time?
  Yes, thanks. Hey, I don't think we've met. I'm Steve Rhodes.
- Hi, are you from around here?
  Yes, I'm from Dallas. How about you?
  No, actually, I'm from Cincinnati. By the way, my name's . . .

Introducing a friend
- Have you met Alan? / Do you know Alan?
  Yes, we've already met.
  No, I haven't. / No, I don't.
- Jill, this is Alan. / I'd you to meet my friend, Alan.
  Hi, Alan. Nice/Good/Pleased to meet you.

Saying farewells
- Goodbye. / Good night.
  See you later. / I'll see you tomorrow.

Clarifying information
- Did you say Davis?
  That's right. / No, Davitz.
- How do you spell that?
  It's D-A-V-I-T-Z.

Unit 2

Talking about family members
- Do you have any brothers or sisters?
  Yes, I have one brother and two sisters.
  No, I'm an only child.
- Are they older or younger than you?
  They're all younger. / They're all older.
  My two sisters are older and my brother is younger.
- Who are the two people on the right?
  Those are my brothers Darryl and Gabe.
- How many people are there in your family?
  Just three: my parents and me.
- Does your sister have any children?
  Yes, she has two sons and a daughter.
  No, she doesn't.
- Is that your father?
  Yes, it is.
  No, it's my uncle.

Giving and responding to compliments
- She's really cute/pretty.
- Wow! He's really handsome.
  Yeah, she/he is.
- I like your hair/dress.
  Thanks. / It's nice of you to notice.

Unit 3

Describing people's appearance
- Eve is young.
- Elaine is middle-aged.
- Paul's tall and kind of heavyset.
- Seiko is average height but she's pretty thin.
- Erika has long hair.
- Peggy's hair is short.
- He has a mustache / beard.
- My father has gray hair. / His hair is gray.
- She has blue eyes. / Her eyes are blue.

Describing people's clothing
- What is she wearing? / What does she have on?
  She / He is wearing a hat / glasses.
  She / He's the one in the blue / black jacket.
- Is that her in the blue T-shirt?
  Yes, that's her.
  No, she's wearing a yellow dress.

Confirming people's identities
- What does she look like?
  She's tall and has short hair.
- Who's the woman in the green dress?
  That's Helen. She's my boss.
- Do you mean the woman in the green hat?
- Is she the one with short blonde hair and glasses?

Yes, that's her.
No, she's the woman with long blonde hair and glasses.
- Is she thin or heavyset?
- Does he have a mustache / beard?
  Yes, he does. / He has a mustache. / He has a beard.
  No, he doesn't. / No, he's clean-shaven.

Hesitating
- Um . . . / Uh . . . / Er . . .
- Let me see . . . / Let's see . . .

Unit 4

Asking for and giving opinions
- What do you think of the new Kelly King album?
- How do you feel about classical music?
  I like it. / It's great.
  I don't mind it. / It's OK.
  I don't like it. / It's terrible.
- Do you like it?
  Yeah, I really like it. / Yeah, it's great.
  No, I can't stand it. / No, it's terrible.
- What do you think?
  It's great.
  It's awful.

Expressing preferences and favorites
- What kind of music do you like?
  All kinds.
  Mostly pop.
- Who do like better, Jenny Hernandez or Tommy Devlin?
  Jenny Hernandez. / I prefer Jenny Hernandez.
  I don't like either one.
- What's your favorite group?
  I like the Glory Hounds.
- I love Aki Matsumura.
  Really? I can't stand her!

Agreeing and disagreeing
- I really like Miles Davis.
  Really? Me too.
  Really? I don't like him.
  Really? I prefer Louis Armstrong.

Expressing surprise
- Really? / You're kidding!
- I don't believe it! / That can't be right!

Unit 5

Asking about and describing places
- What's New York like?
  It's a really exciting place to visit but it's pretty expensive.
- Is Los Angeles a safe place to live?
  Yes, it's very safe.
  No, I don't think so. / No, not really.
- Have you ever been to China?
  Yes, I've been to Shanghai.
  No, I haven't. / No, I've never been there.

Clarifying personal information
- You're from Singapore, aren't you?
  Yes, I am.
  Actually, I'm from Malaysia.
- Are you still living in San Francisco?
  Yes, I am. / Yes, I'm still there.
  No, I live in Oakland now.
- Are you American? / You're American, aren't you?
  Yes, I am.
  No, I'm Australian.

Showing realization
- Oh yeah. / Yeah, you're right. / Oh, I didn't know that.

Unit 6

Talking about apartments
- Is it furnished?
  Yes, it is. / Yes, it's fully furnished.
  No, it's unfurnished.
  It's partially furnished.
- Does it come with a washer and dryer?
  Yes, it does.
  No, it doesn't. / No, those aren't included.
- Is there a balcony?

Yes, there's a balcony off the living room.
No, there isn't.
- How much is the rent? / What's the rent?
  It's $600 a month.

Talking about quantity
- How many rooms does it have?
  Five. / It's a two-bedroom. / It's a five-room apartment.
- There are six rooms altogether.
- It has three bedrooms, two bathrooms, a kitchen and a living room.

Expressing satisfaction
- Looks great! / It looks really comfortable. / It's really nice.

Expressing disappointment
- Oh, no. / Oh, that's too bad. / I'm sorry to hear that.

Unit 7

Asking about locations in a store
- Is there a sporting goods department?
  Yes, it's on the second floor, next to the elevators.
  No, there isn't.
- Where are the restrooms?
  They're on the third floor next to the women's wear department.
- What floor are the VCRs on?
  They're on the third floor in the electronics department.
- Can you tell me where to find women's shoes?
  Take the elevator/escalator to the fourth floor.

Expressing and responding to thanks
- Thanks. / Thank you. / Thanks a lot.
  You're welcome. / Don't mention it. / No problem. / That's OK.

Unit 8

Talking about abilities

- Can you use DesignWiz?
  Yes, I can. I can also use PictureShop.
  No, I can't. But I'm a fast learner.
- Have you ever used Exalt 2.0?
  Yes, I have. I used it in my last job.
  No, I haven't. But I've used AccPac.

Talking about job preferences

- Is earning a high salary important to you?
  Yes, it's very important.
  No, job satisfaction is more important.
- Do you prefer to work alone or on a team?
  I prefer to work alone.

Checking understanding

- Do you understand? / Do you know what I mean?
  Yes, I do.
  No, I don't.

Asking about language ability

- Can you speak Spanish?
  Yes, I can.
  I can speak a little.
  No, but I can speak German.

Unit 9

Asking for and offering help

- Sorry. Could I ask you a question? / Excuse me, would you mind helping me?
  Sure, no problem. / Sure, what can I do for you?
  Sorry, I'm in a hurry. / I'd like to but I'm in a hurry.
- Can I help you find something? / You look a little lost. Can I help you?
  Thanks. I'm looking for a bank. / Yeah, I'm looking for the post office.

Asking for and giving directions

- I'm looking for a good place to have dinner.
- Excuse me, is there a restaurant nearby?/Are there any restaurants around here?
  Yes, there's one/some on 43rd Street.
  No, there's not. / No, there isn't.
- Do you know how to get to the park? / How do I get to the park?
  Go up Queen Street to 33rd Avenue and turn right.

Asking for and giving recommendations

- Could you recommend a hotel in the area? / Do you know any good hotels around here? / Where's a good hotel?
  You could try the Royal Aston. / The Hilltop Hotel is right around the corner.
- Are there any nice parks in the city?
  Kowloon Park is nice.

Describing places in a city

- The drugstore is next to the post office.
- There's a market on Church Street, across from the park.
- The supermarket is between the hotel and the subway station.
- The hotel is on Dundas Street.

Unit 10

Asking for and giving instructions

- Do you know how this works? / Can you show me how this works?
  Sure. First, press the 'Start' button. Then, move the cursor to 'Programs.' Finally, click on the 'e' icon.
  Sorry, I don't know how it works either.
- What do I do first?
  First you have to turn it on.
- How do I adjust the focus? / How do I focus it?
  Press and hold this button.

Asking for confirmation

- Do I press here to open it?
  Yes, that's the one.
  No, don't press that one. Press the one that says 'Connect.'
- Which button do I press? / Which one is it?
  The 'Eject' button. / The one that says 'Eject.'

Unit 11

Talking about times and daily routines

- What time do you usually get up in the morning?
  I get up at about 7:30.
- When do you usually have lunch/dinner?
  Usually at about 12:30. / From about noon to one.
  I usually have dinner at about eight.
- What do you do after school?
  I go to the gym, then go home and have dinner.
- How much TV do you watch every day?
  About three hours. / I watch TV for about three hours.

Unit 12

Ordering food

- Would you like to see a menu?
  Yes, please.
  No, thanks. I'll just have a coffee.
- What would you like to order?
  I'd like the T-bone steak.
- How would you like that done?
  Medium rare/medium/well done, please.
- What kind of dressing would you like?
  I'll have Italian. / Italian, please.
- What would you like to drink? / Would you like something to drink? / Anything to drink?
  I'll have an iced tea. / Iced tea, please.

- Would you like anything else?
  Yes, could I have a piece of apple pie, please?
  No, that's all. / That will do it.

Confirming food orders
- Did you say large cola?
  Yes. That's right.
  No, medium, please.
- That comes with French fries, right?
  Yes, it does.
  It comes with a choice of French fries or baked potato.
  No, I'm afraid it doesn't. / No, I'm sorry, It doesn't.
- So that's two coffees and two pieces of cake?
  Yes, that's right.
  No, two coffees and one piece of cake.

Making reservations
- I'd like to reserve a table on Saturday. / I'd like to make a reservation for Saturday.
- I'd like to reserve a table for tomorrow, please. / Can I book a table for tomorrow?
  At what time? / What time would you like? /What time will you be arriving?
  For how many people, please? / How many in your party?
  Sorry, we're fully booked that night.

Unit 13

Talking about sports preferences
- Do you watch a lot of sports on TV?
  Yeah, I watch sports just about every day.
  Not really.
- Do you play much golf?
  Yes, I play every weekend.
  No, I hardly ever play.
- Have you ever played football?
  Yes, I played it in high school.
  No. Never.

- What's your favorite baseball team? / Who's your favorite baseball player?
  The New York Yankees. / Ichiro Suzuki.
  I don't really have a favorite.
- Which do you like better, tennis or badminton?
  Tennis. / I prefer tennis.
  I don't really like either one.

Talking about frequency
- How often to you go to soccer games?
  I go about once a month.
  Never.
- Do you play tennis on the weekend?
  Yes, I play every Sunday morning.
  No, just on Tuesdays.

Unit 14

Offering, accepting and declining invitations
- Do you want to see a movie tonight? / Let's see a movie tonight?
- I have two concert tickets for tonight. Want to go?
- Would you like to have dinner tonight?
  Sure. / Yeah, I'd love to. / Sounds great. / Alright.
  Sorry, I can't make it that night. / I'm not really interested. / Sorry, I have plans.
  I'd like to, but I have to study. / I'd rather go tomorrow night.

Apologizing and responding to apologies
- Sorry. / Sorry about that.
  Don't mention it. / It's alright. / Don't worry about it. / It's no problem.

Unit 15

Talking about the weather
- What's the weather like? / How's the weather?

It's hot and sunny. / It's really cold.
- It looks like rain.
- What's the temperature?
  It's about 33 degrees / minus 10 / 10 below.
- What's the forecast for this weekend?
  It's supposed to rain on Saturday.
- Is it cold outside?
  Yeah, it's freezing.
  No, it's warm.

Unit 16

Describing appearance and personality
- Could you describe your appearance for me? / What do you look like?
  I'm kind of tall with brown hair.
- Would you say you're average height?
  I think so.
  No, actually I'm kind of short.
- Would you say you're a shy person?
  Yes, I guess I am.
  No, I'm pretty/kind of outgoing.

Introducing a story/narrative
- As a matter of fact . . . / Actually . . . / You won't believe this . . .

Talking about dating and relationships
- I'm looking for someone who likes to have fun.
- The person I meet should like going to concerts.

Talking about past events
- What did you do last weekend?
  We went to a movie on Saturday night and just stayed in on Sunday.

Unit 17

Making suggestions
- Why don't we buy a new car?
- How about having the wedding in May?

- Let's go out for dinner tonight.
- I think we should go to Chicago.

Accepting suggestions
- That sounds good. / Alright. / Great. / Yeah, OK. / That's a good idea.

Rejecting suggestions
- I don't think so. / I'd prefer a different one.
- No, that one is too small. / I'd rather not.
- I don't really want to. / Thanks, but I have other plans. / I'd like to but I'm busy that day

Unit 18

Describing personality
- How would you describe yourself?
  I think I'm a hardworking person.
- What's your new boyfriend like?
  He's kind of quiet and shy.

Asking for reasons
- How come? / Why is that? / Did she say why?

Unit 19

Describing and confirming appointments
- Are you doing anything on Monday night?
  Yes, I have a date.
  No, I'm free that night.
- Are you free this Thursday?
  Yeah, my schedule is wide open.
  I've got a doctor's appointment at eleven but I'm free after that.
  No, I'm having dinner with my parents.
- Are we still playing tennis on Sunday?
  Yeah, I'll see you at the club at ten.
  Sorry, I can't. I have to work that morning.

Changing and canceling appointments
- Sorry, I can't make it that day. Something came up.
- The coach is sick so practice is cancelled.
- The meeting was supposed to be at four but now it's at five.
- Would you mind if we went out another night?

Unit 20

Talking about learning preferences
- How did you learn to use your cell phone?
  I read the instruction manual.
- What's the last book you read for fun?
  The Summons by John Grisham.
- How do you study for a test?
  I rewrite my notes several times.
- What was your favorite class at school?
  I really liked gym class.
- Do you prefer to read a textbook or listen to a lecture?
  I prefer listening to a lecture.

Listening Skills Index

Self-Study Practice Units

Welcome to the Self Study Practice section of *Listen In*. This section of the book will give you extra practice with the target language and listening strategies used in the main units of *Listen In*. In order to complete the Self-Study Practice section, you need to use the Self-Study Practice CD on the inside back cover of this book.

The Self-Study Practice section is made up of 20 separate units. Each one-page unit has the same titles, goals, and target language as one of the 20 main units of *Listen In*. The units in the Self-Study Practice section should be completed one at a time, and only after you have covered the material in the matching main unit in class.

Each unit in the Self-Study Practice section consists of two tasks. The listening passage for each task is recorded on a separate track of the Self-Study Practice CD. See page 128 for a full listing of the CD tracks.

Here is what to do for every unit in the Self-Study Practice section:

Task 1, Part A: There are six questions or statements on the Self-Study Practice CD for this section. For each one, you will find three possible responses listed on the page. Read the list of responses and then listen to the CD. Decide which is the best response for each question or statement and circle the letter (a, b, or c).

For example, you hear:
1. *Excuse me. Are you Jason Lee?*

You see:
1. **a.** Nice to meet you, Jason.
   b. No, I'm Terry Phillips.
   c. Hi, Mr. Lee.

The best response is *No, I'm Terry Phillips.*, so for this question you should circle 'b.'

Task 1, Part B: Listen to the questions or statements again, along with the correct response to each one. Check to make sure your answers are correct.

Task 2, Part A: The listening passage is a longer dialog or monolog, such as a conversation, an announcement, or a radio broadcast. First, read the instructions and the questions you need to answer. Each unit features one of three question types: (1) Listen and circle the best answer, (2) Listen and circle *T* for *True* or *F* for *False*, and (3) Listen and match the names with the titles. Think about what kind of information you will need to listen for. Then listen and complete your answers.

Task 2, Part B: Carefully read the instructions. Think about what type of information you need to listen for (names, descriptions, locations, etc.) and how you need to fill in your answers (filling in a chart, map, menu, survey, etc.). Play the dialog or monolog in Part A again and complete your answers.

Some listening tips:
- Complete the Self-Study Practice section in a quiet place with no distractions.
- Try to predict the words you need to listen for and make a list before you begin.
- Don't try to understand every word, just listen for the information you need.
- If you don't get all the information after listening twice, play the track again.

Good luck!

UNIT 1

Pleased to meet you.

TASK 1

Student CD Track: 2

A Listen and circle the best response.

1. a. Yes, it is.
   b. No, I'm not.
   c. Teacher.

2. a. No, it's Phil.
   b. Yes, I am.
   c. Yes, it is.

3. a. Yes, I am.
   b. She's studying.
   c. No, English.

4. a. Yes, I am.
   b. No, I don't.
   c. Yes, she is.

5. a. My last name.
   b. That's right.
   c. I think so.

6. a. Pleased to meet you.
   b. Are you Janet?
   c. Do you know Janet?

B Listen again and check your answers.

TASK 2

Student CD Track: 3

A Listen and circle the best answer.

1. This is . . .
   a. a face-to-face conversation.
   b. an answering machine message.
   c. a telephone conversation.

2. Judy . . .
   a. can't come to the party.
   b. can come to the party.
   c. is having a house party.

3. Tom . . .
   a. plans to invite guests by phone.
   b. plans to send out invitations.
   c. plans to invite Judy to the party.

B Who does Tom plan to invite? Listen again and write the names.

Guest List

Judy Fletcher

UNIT

This is my family.

Student CD Track: 4

A Listen and circle the best response.

1. a. No, we're not brothers.
   b. No, just sisters.
   c. No, he's my uncle.

2. a. Yes, it is.
   b. I have a wife.
   c. Yes, I do.

3. a. Do you have a daughter?
   b. My son is ten.
   c. How old is she?

4. a. Two.
   b. I'm the oldest.
   c. Yes, I do.

5. a. My brother.
   b. My aunt and uncle.
   c. They sure are.

6. a. Do you really?
   b. Are you really?
   c. Can you really?

B Listen again and check your answers.

Student CD Track: 5

A Read the statements. Then listen and circle *T* for *True* or *F* for *False*.

1. Allie has a younger sister.   T   F
2. Maggie is Allie's niece.   T   F

3. Michelle is Allie's sister.   T   F
4. Danny is Allie's son.   T   F

B Listen again and complete Allie's family tree.

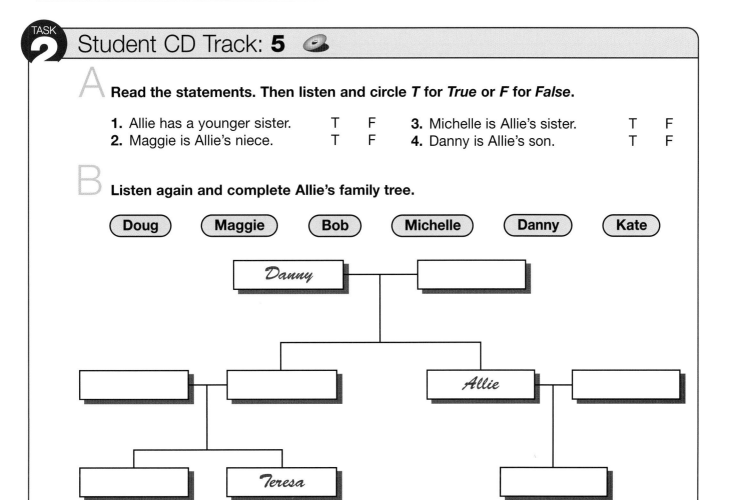

Doug   Maggie   Bob   Michelle   Danny   Kate

UNIT 3

He's the one in the blue shirt.

Student CD Track: 6

A **Listen and circle the best response.**

1. a. No, he's not my
   father.
   b. No, he's my uncle.
   c. No, my brother is tall.

2. a. Yes, I wear glasses.
   b. Do you wear glasses?
   c. Yes, I see her.

3. a. She's the one in the
   green shirt.
   b. He's over there.
   c. It's my sister.

4. a. Yes, she is.
   b. I don't know.
   c. She's wearing a jacket.

5. a. Oh, I see him.
   b. Is that her over there?
   c. Does he have a
   mustache?

6. a. Does he have red
   hair?
   b. No, he isn't.
   c. Yes, it is.

B **Listen again and check your answers.**

Student CD Track: 7

A **Listen and circle the best answer.**

1. **The movie director is
   talking with . . .**
   a. an actor.
   b. an agent.
   c. a director.

2. **The director wants . . .**
   a. three big movie stars.
   b. three million dollars.
   c. three regular actors.

3. **He is looking for . . .**
   a. three men.
   b. two men and a
   woman.
   c. two women and a
   man.

B **What do the actors have to look like? Listen again and circle the correct
description for each.**

	M/W	Age	Height	Build	Hair Color
Actor #1	Man	Young	Tall	Heavyset	Brown
	Woman	Middle-aged	Average height	Average	Blond(e)
		Old	Short	Thin	Red
Actor #2	Man	Young	Tall	Heavyset	Brown
	Woman	Middle-aged	Average height	Average	Blond(e)
		Old	Short	Thin	Red
Actor #3	Man	Young	Tall	Heavyset	Brown
	Woman	Middle-aged	Average height	Average	Blond(e)
		Old	Short	Thin	Red

Do you like rock?

UNIT

 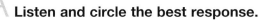

Student CD Track: **8**

A **Listen and circle the best response.**

1. a. No, she doesn't.
   b. I prefer classical.
   c. Yes, I do.

2. a. It's OK.
   b. No, I don't.
   c. I can't stand jazz.

3. a. No, it's jazz that I like.
   b. I don't like rock.
   c. I don't mind it.

4. a. Classical.
   b. I prefer music.
   c. I like some of his songs.

5. a. No, I don't.
   b. I don't know. I just don't.
   c. I don't like rock music.

6. a. I love it.
   b. No, I don't.
   c. Me too. She's great.

B **Listen again and check your answers.**

Student CD Track: **9**

A **Listen and match the artists with the awards.**

1. B3   3. Candy Warner   5. Horn of Plenty

2. Tessa Traynor   4. The Castaways

Best Rock Band: _____   Best Pop Album: _____   Best New Artist: _____
Song of the Year: _____   Best Dance Album: _____

B **Listen again. What does Marcia think of the musicians? Check the correct column for each.**

	Likes	Doesn't mind	Doesn't like
B3			
Candy Warner			
Horn of Plenty			
Tessa Traynor			
The Castaways			

UNIT 5

It's a really interesting place.

TASK 1

Student CD Track: **10**

A Listen and circle the best response.

1. **a.** Taipei.
   b. Yeah, that's right.
   c. I'm from Taipei.

2. **a.** New York, actually.
   b. Yes, she does.
   c. Yes, I am.

3. **a.** Yes, it is.
   b. Yes, I do.
   c. Yes, I am.

4. **a.** No, I'm not.
   b. Yes, it is.
   c. Seoul.

5. **a.** Yes, it is.
   b. Big.
   c. I like big cities

6. **a.** Yeah, but it's quite expensive.
   b. Yeah, but it's really exciting.
   c. Yeah, but I'm sure you'd like it.

B Listen again and check your answers.

TASK 2

Student CD Track: **11**

A Read the statements. Then listen and circle *T* for *True* or *F* for *False*.

1. Min-hee is thinking about taking a vacation in the United States.   T   F
2. Evan has been to all three cities.   T   F
3. Evan's hometown is San Francisco.   T   F
4. Min-hee has been to San Francisco.   T   F
5. Min-hee doesn't know much about the schools.   T   F

B Listen again. Check (✔) the words Evan uses to describe each city.

City	beautiful	clean	exciting	expensive	interesting	modern	quiet
San Francisco							
Salt Lake City							
Boston							

This is where I live.

UNIT

TASK 1

Student CD Track: **12**

A Listen and circle the best response.

1. a. Next to the bedroom.
   b. Yes, it does.
   c. Two.

2. a. Yes, and it's really comfortable.
   b. Yes, and the view is great.
   c. Yes, it's in the bedroom.

3. a. No, it doesn't.
   b. Yes, it does.
   c. Yes, there is.

4. a. Two months' rent.
   b. $600 a month.
   c. It has two bathrooms.

5. a. It's close to the beach.
   b. It's expensive.
   c. Yes, it is.

6. a. They're moving.
   b. Yes, you can.
   c. Next month.

B Listen again and check your answers.

TASK 2

Student CD Track: **13**

A Listen and circle the best answer.

1. This is . . .
   a. a TV commercial.
   b. a telephone answering machine message.
   c. a radio ad.

2. The apartment has . . .
   a. two bedrooms.
   b. three bedrooms.
   c. four bedrooms.

3. The apartment is . . .
   a. close to the city.
   b. close to the mountains.
   c. close to the beach.

B Look at the floor plans. Listen again and check (✔) the correct apartment.

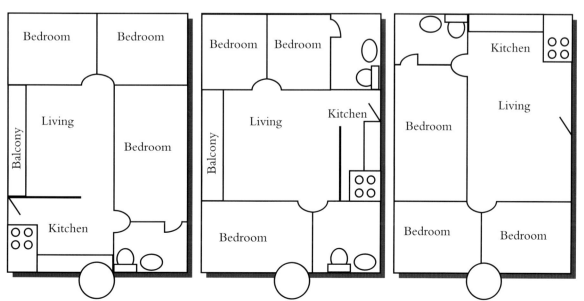

UNIT

It's on the third floor.

A Listen and circle the best response.

1. **a.** Sporting goods? On the second floor.
   b. It's next to the sporting goods department.
   c. No, I don't see them.

2. **a.** Yes, this is the women's wear department.
   b. Children's wear is on the fourth floor.
   c. No, it's on the fourth floor.

3. **a.** Next to the toy department.
   b. The electrical goods department.
   c. Electrical goods are on the fifth floor.

4. **a.** I'm looking for the restrooms.
   b. Yes, there's a restaurant on the fourth floor.
   c. Yes, they're next to the travel goods department.

5. **a.** Women's wear and shoes.
   b. Women's wear is on sale.
   c. Women's wear is on the second floor.

6. **a.** No, there are no toys in sporting goods.
   b. No, but there's a toy store across the street.
   c. No, Dad is in the toy department.

B Listen again and check your answers.

A Listen and circle the best answer.

1. The man is talking to . . .
   a. his son.
   b. his wife.
   c. a store clerk.

2. The conversation takes place in . . .
   a. the shoe department.
   b. a department store.
   c. a toy store.

3. The man wants to buy . . .
   a. children's shoes.
   b. sporting goods.
   c. women's shoes.

B Listen again and label the places in the store.

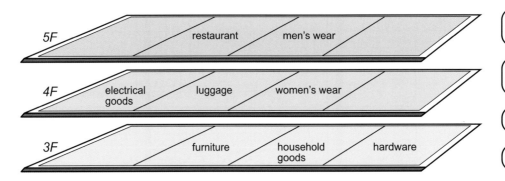

children's shoes

sporting goods

toys

restrooms

UNIT

Can you work weekends?

Student CD Track: 16

A **Listen and circle the best response.**

1. a. I'm a teacher.
   b. Are you a teacher?
   c. Falls City High School.

2. a. As a waiter.
   b. Hudson Accounting.
   c. Monday to Friday.

3. a. Yes, I like it.
   b. For two years.
   c. Yes, I can.

4. a. Carlson Street.
   b. The hours are long.
   c. For about three years.

5. a. I don't know.
   b. Yes, I speak Spanish.
   c. I can write it.

6. a. 40 words a minute.
   b. Yes, I can type.
   c. $40 an hour.

B **Listen again and check your answers.**

Student CD Track: 17

A **Listen and circle the best answer.**

1. **Lucy asks about a . . .**
   a. newspaper interview.
   b. job interview.
   c. college interview.

2. **Lucy's appointment is for . . .**
   a. 2:00.
   b. 2:30.
   c. 2:45.

3. **Lucy talks to . . .**
   a. Paula.
   b. Barbara.
   c. Conrad.

B **Listen again and circle Lucy's answers.**

Name: *Lucy Turner*		
Position wanted:	Editor	Designer	Writer
Computer skills:	PictureShop	DesignWiz	Exalt 2.0
Languages:	French	German	Japanese
Availability:	Days	Evenings	Weekends

UNIT 9

Where's the ferry terminal?

TASK 1

Student CD Track: 18

A Listen and circle the best response.

1. a. I'm going shopping.
    b. It's next to the ferry terminal.
    c. Yes, there is.

2. a. Yes, we do.
    b. It's near the hotel.
    c. Yes, there's one on Ridge Road.

3. a. Go to Third Avenue and turn right.
    b. Yes, there's a park near here.
    c. The park opens at nine.

4. a. The museum is on the right.
    b. For about two years.
    c. At 10:00.

5. a. No, the hotel is open.
    b. No, it's right across the street.
    c. No, it's a hotel.

6. a. It's close to the hotel.
    b. Italian food.
    c. There are some on Watt Street.

B Listen again and check your answers.

TASK 2

Student CD Track: 19

A Listen and circle the best answer.

1. **This is a guide to . . .**
   a. hotels.
   b. shopping centers.
   c. museums.

2. **This announcement is for . . .**
   a. city residents.
   b. tourists.
   c. airport workers.

3. **The shuttle bus is going to . . .**
   a. downtown Metropolis.
   b. downtown Merrimack.
   c. downtown Kandor.

B Listen again and label the hotels on the map.

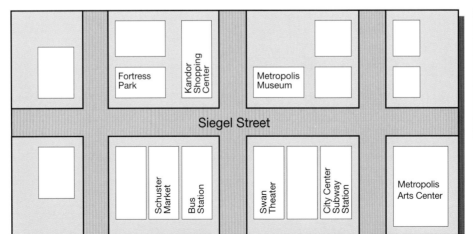

UNIT

How does it work?

Student CD Track: **20**

A **Listen and circle the best response.**

1. **a.** It's a computer.
   b. First, you plug it in.
   c. Yes, it does.

2. **a.** It opens the cover.
   b. Press the 'power' button.
   c. You have to turn it on.

3. **a.** Yes, you do.
   b. Here is the cassette.
   c. Put it in here.

4. **a.** This is the 'off' button.
   b. No, over here.
   c. Yes, it is.

5. **a.** Just press this button.
   b. Don't turn it on.
   c. Take out the tape.

6. **a.** That's the next step.
   b. Yes, you do.
   c. Click on an icon.

B **Listen again and check your answers.**

Student CD Track: **21**

A **Listen and circle the best answer.**

1. **This is a conversation between . . .**
   a. two co-workers.
   b. two friends.
   c. two teachers.

2. **PictureDisc is . . .**
   a. a CD-ROM.
   b. a web site.
   c. a newsletter.

3. **Pete describes how to . . .**
   a. use a camera to take a photo.
   b. download a photo from the Internet.
   c. design a new web site.

B **Listen again and number the instructions (2–7). One instruction is extra.**

_____ Click on the photo.

_____ Insert the disk in your computer.

_____ Type a file name.

_____ Use the Search Engine to look for photos.

_1_ Type your name and employee number.

_____ Press 'Save' to store it on your computer.

_____ Open the catalog page.

_____ Choose 'Save Picture As . . .'

UNIT

I usually get up at six.

 TASK 1

Student CD Track: 22

A Listen and circle the best response.

1. **a.** Yes, I do.
   b. Every day.
   c. Around four-thirty.

2. **a.** At 9:00.
   b. I get to school about 9:00.
   c. Yes, they usually do.

3. **a.** I'm busy this Saturday.
   b. I eat lunch.
   c. I clean the house.

4. **a.** About forty-five minutes.
   b. Twelve-thirty.
   c. Soup and a sandwich.

5. **a.** Not usually.
   b. On Wednesday night.
   c. No, I don't.

6. **a.** After five.
   b. Never.
   c. Any time.

B Listen again and check your answers.

 TASK 2

Student CD Track: 23

A Listen and circle the best answer.

1. **The conversation is between a . . .**
   a. student and his friend.
   b. student and his father.
   c. student and a school counselor.

2. **The conversation is about . . .**
   a. school sports.
   b. managing time better.
   c. tomorrow's schedule.

3. **Paul agrees to . . .**
   a. stop volunteering.
   b. stop playing soccer.
   c. stop working at the supermarket.

B Listen again and fill in Paul's daily schedule.

(volunteer work)　(get up)　(classes start)　(soccer practice)

(part-time job)　(watches TV)　(homework)

8:00	3:00	9:00
9:00	↓ 4:00	11:00
noon	5:00	↓ 1:00
↓　volunteer work 1:00	↓ 8:00	

Self Study Practice

I'll have soup and a sandwich.

Student CD Track: **24**

A **Listen and circle the best response**

1. **a.** I'd like a hot dog, please.
   b. Yes, please.
   c. Yes, I already ordered.

2. **a.** What kind would you like?
   b. Small or large?
   c. Anything else?

3. **a.** No, French fries, please.
   b. Medium rare.
   c. No, thanks.

4. **a.** Root beer, please.
   b. A drink.
   c. Medium, please.

5. **a.** Sorry, we're full tonight.
   b. How many people?
   c. Around seven o'clock.

6. **a.** No, the cheeseburger.
   b. Will that be all?
   c. Here's your hamburger.

B **Listen again and check your answers.**

Student CD Track: **25**

A **Listen and circle *T* for *True*, *F* for *False*, or *U* for *Unknown*.**

1. Sally is ordering a meal over the phone.	T	F	U
2. She is ordering breakfast.	T	F	U
3. She orders a salad.	T	F	U
4. She will order dessert.	T	F	U

B **Listen again and check (✔) Sally's order.**

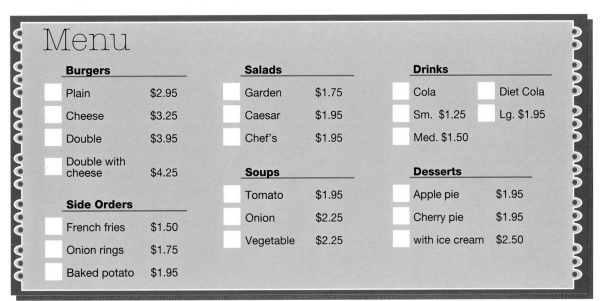

Menu

Burgers		
☐ Plain	$2.95	
☐ Cheese	$3.25	
☐ Double	$3.95	
☐ Double with cheese	$4.25	

Side Orders	
☐ French fries	$1.50
☐ Onion rings	$1.75
☐ Baked potato	$1.95

Salads	
☐ Garden	$1.75
☐ Caesar	$1.95
☐ Chef's	$1.95

Soups	
☐ Tomato	$1.95
☐ Onion	$2.25
☐ Vegetable	$2.25

Drinks	
☐ Cola	☐ Diet Cola
☐ Sm. $1.25	☐ Lg. $1.95
☐ Med. $1.50	

Desserts	
☐ Apple pie	$1.95
☐ Cherry pie	$1.95
☐ with ice cream	$2.50

He shoots, he scores!

  Student CD Track: **26**

A **Listen and circle the best response.**

1. a. Yes, I can.
   b. Do you?
   c. Yes, I do.

2. a. I like it, too.
   b. Really? That's great.
   c. Sometimes.

3. a. The gym.
   b. Yes, I do.
   c. Hardly ever.

4. a. I can play on Tuesday.
   b. The golf course.
   c. No, I don't know how.

5. a. How about tomorrow?
   b. I'm not bad.
   c. Do you play?

6. a. Do you? I think it's boring.
   b. So can I.
   c. Every day.

B **Listen again and check your answers.**

Student CD Track: **27**

A **Listen and circle the best answer.**

1. The speaker is a . . .
   a. sports coach.
   b. radio reporter.
   c. basketball player.

2. He is describing a . . .
   a. soccer game.
   b. volleyball game.
   c. basketball game.

3. The winning team is . . .
   a. England.
   b. Spain.
   c. Germany.

B **Listen again. Fill in the team of each player who scored, and the time they scored.**

Player	Team	Time
Garcia	_____	_____
Lockhart	_____	_____
Salazar	_____	_____
Gonzalez	_____	_____
Gregson	_____	_____

UNIT

Do you want to see a movie?

TASK 1

Student CD Track: 28

A **Listen and circle the best response.**

1. a. OK. How about having seafood?
   b. No, I'm busy tomorrow night.
   c. Sure. What movies are playing?

2. a. I watched TV.
   b. Yeah, sounds good.
   c. I don't really like to dance.

3. a. That's great. When is it?
   b. Yes, I can.
   c. I don't like classical music.

4. a. No, thanks. I'm busy.
   b. How about Sharkey's?
   c. What time does it start?

5. a. Oh, I've seen it.
   b. I usually stay home.
   c. The movie theater is on Pearl Street.

6. a. I love basketball.
   b. No, I don't.
   c. I'd rather go to the art gallery.

B **Listen again and check your answers.**

TASK 2

Student CD Track: 29

A **Listen and circle *T* for *True*, *F* for *False*, or *U* for *Unknown*.**

1. Wendy likes modern art.   T   F   U
2. Cliff has seen *Call to Action*.   T   F   U
3. Wendy doesn't like Purple Sage.   T   F   U
4. They decide to see a concert.   T   F   U

B **Listen again and circle the things they discuss.**

•[Entertainment guide]•

Purple Sage Rides Again!
Reunion show at Mosley Hall
8 P.M. Saturday

Japanese Film Festival
All week long at the Broadway Cinema

All-night Techno Party
Every Saturday at Ichabod's
Doors open at 10 P.M.

Live at Kind of Blue!
The Kerry Gammill Band
Show starts at 9 P.M.

Blake Claymore in Call to Action!
Nightly at the Hillcrest Cineplex
Matinees Sat. & Sun.

Rosewood Gallery
An Exhibition of Modern Art
by The X/S Group
Aug. 18–Sep. 13

Ellen Aim & the Attackers
Opening act: Cliffhangers
Live at Call the Office, 9 P.M.

Kendall's Folly
See the award-winning Broadway
play. Runs until Sep. 27

What's the weather like?

TASK 1 Student CD Track: 30

A Listen and circle the best response.

1. **a.** Yes, I know it is.
   b. Yes, it's going to be warm.
   c. Yes, it rains a lot.

2. **a.** Great. I'm going to the beach today.
   b. No, I heard it's going to rain.
   c. I'd better take an umbrella.

3. **a.** It's really hot.
   b. Yes, it is.
   c. I really like snowy weather.

4. **a.** Yeah, I heard that, too.
   b. Good. I like when it rains.
   c. Let's go swimming.

5. **a.** It's cloudy outside.
   b. Have you seen my umbrella?
   c. Really? I thought it was quite cold.

6. **a.** Yeah, it's going to be sunny.
   b. I wore my winter coat yesterday.
   c. I don't like it either.

B Listen again and check your answers.

TASK 2 Student CD Track: 31

A Listen and circle the best answer.

1. **This is a weather report for . . .**
   a. today.
   b. tomorrow.
   c. the weekend.

2. **Rain is forecast in . . .**
   a. London, Paris, Madrid.
   b. Rome, Madrid, Paris.
   c. Paris, Rome, Athens.

3. **Travelers will need a sweater in . . .**
   a. Athens.
   b. Madrid.
   c. London.

B Listen again. Write temperatures next to the cities and draw symbols to show the weather.

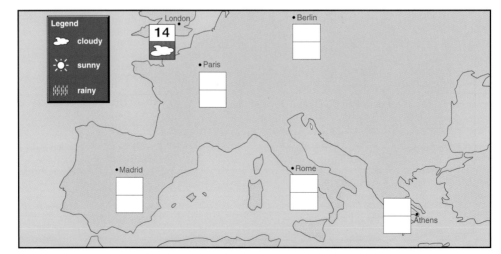

How did you meet your wife?

Student CD Track: **32**

A **Listen and circle the best response.**

1. a. She's kind of tall with brown hair.
    b. Yes, she does.
    c. She likes music.

2. a. Through a dating agency.
    b. About four years ago.
    c. He's an accountant.

3. a. Someone who's outgoing.
    b. Yes, I guess I'm outgoing.
    c. I'm going out now.

4. a. She likes music and going to parties.
    b. Yes, I am. Do you know Jeff Lim?
    c. Yes, it's on the eighteenth.

5. a. Not really.
    b. So do I.
    c. Oh, really? What kind of sports?

6. a. You'd like my sister. She's really funny.
    b. You'd like my sister. She plays badminton, too.
    c. You'd like my sister. She's quite tall.

B **Listen again and check your answers.**

Student CD Track: **33**

A **Listen and circle *T* for *True*, *F* for *False*, or *U* for *Unknown*.**

1. She plays tennis twice a week.	T	F	U
2. She lives with her parents.	T	F	U
3. She likes animals.	T	F	U
4. She has short hair.	T	F	U

B **Listen again and fill in the form.**

Name: *Juliet A. Eastman*

Age: _____

Hair: black   brown   blonde   red

Eyes: gray   brown   blue   green

Height: tall   average   short

Occupation: _____

Likes: _____

Wants to meet someone who: _____

UNIT 17

Why don't we buy a new car?

Student CD Track: **34**

A Listen and circle the best response.

1. **a.** I've seen it.
   b. It's too expensive.
   c. It's too far away.

2. **a.** I've seen it.
   b. I'd prefer to see a movie.
   c. Sounds good.

3. **a.** I'm a little short of money.
   b. I think he's out.
   c. I think it's going to rain.

4. **a.** OK. Where shall we go?
   b. OK. Have you seen the new movie at the Odeon?
   c. OK. Let's just stay home.

5. **a.** It's not too cold.
   b. That's too bad.
   c. They're out of town this weekend.

6. **a.** It's too hot.
   b. Are they free tonight?
   c. Oh, but it's so boring!

B Listen again and check your answers.

Student CD Track: **35**

A Listen and circle the best answer.

1. **This is a conversation between . . .**
   a. two friends.
   b. two co-workers.
   c. a married couple.

2. **They are planning where to go . . .**
   a. for lunch tomorrow.
   b. for dinner tonight.
   c. for dinner tomorrow night.

3. **They . . .**
   a. agree on a place to go.
   b. don't agree on a place to go.
   c. decide to do something different.

B Listen again. Number the places (1–5) with the objections you hear.

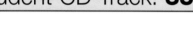

Dining Out

○ **Kurama Japanese Emporium**
Your #1 choice for sushi
Located at 161 112th Avenue
Reservations: 555 8484

○ **Experience 'Provence!'**
Fine French Cuisine
16-A 8th Avenue S.
Tel: 555 0440

○ **For a Taste of India**
Come to The Taj!
At the Crown Hotel

○ **Luigi's Italian Eatery**
120 Davis Square
Tel: 555 4890

○ **Hutch's Hot Dog Café**
Try our Jumbo Chili Dogs!
City Core Mall, tel: 555 1975

○ **Chimichanga's Mexican Food**
764 Central Avenue
Tel: 555 7765

1. I've already been there.
2. I've heard the food's bad.
3. It looks expensive.
4. I don't like really hot food.
5. It's too far away.

UNIT 18

She's kind of shy.

TASK 1   Student CD Track: **36**

A **Listen and circle the best response.**

1. a. He started last week.
   b. He's new.
   c. He seems OK.

2. a. She's over there.
   b. Really annoying.
   c. She likes rap music.

3. a. What, the noisy one? Yeah, that's him.
   b. Uh-huh. She's just over there.
   c. He's OK, but he's really noisy.

4. a. Have you met them?
   b. Don't worry, they're really friendly.
   c. Yeah. They're really nice, aren't they?

5. a. Yes, she's really outgoing.
   b. Only when we're with other people.
   c. We're about the same age.

6. a. I'd say I was a bit lazy.
   b. Is she outgoing?
   c. Someone who's hardworking and smart.

B **Listen again and check your answers.**

TASK 2   Student CD Track: **37**

A **Listen and circle the best answer.**

1. **Kylie is talking to . . .**
   a. her sister.
   b. her teacher.
   c. her boss.

2. **The survey is from . . .**
   a. a book.
   b. a magazine.
   c. a newspaper.

3. **According to the survey, she is . . .**
   a. a snake.
   b. a sheep.
   c. a pig.

B **Look at the survey questions. Listen again and check (✔) Kylie's answers.**

Your True Personality Revealed

1. **At parties, . . .**
   _____ I like to introduce myself to strangers.
   _____ I like to wait until people come and talk to me.

2. **In social situations, . . .**
   _____ I am quiet.
   _____ I am talkative.

3. **At sporting events, . . .**
   _____ I like to cheer loudly for my team.
   _____ I prefer to stay silent, even when my team is winning.

4. **At work, . . .**
   _____ I feel comfortable chatting with the boss.
   _____ I feel uncomfortable if I have to talk to the boss.

125

Are you free on Tuesday?

Student CD Track: **38**

A Listen and circle the best response.

1. a. No, not really.
   b. Yes, I'm free all day.
   c. It's tomorrow.

2. a. It's on Monday.
   b. Pretty full.
   c. It's from 6:00.

3. a. Every weekend.
   b. Tuesday and Thursday.
   c. Friday morning.

4. a. Great. Let's go see a movie.
   b. Are you busy then?
   c. That's too bad.

5. a. What time is that?
   b. Oh, I forgot.
   c. But I have to go out in the evening.

6. a. When does it start?
   b. Are you going?
   c. Oh, really? Why?

B Listen again and check your answers.

Student CD Track: **39**

A Listen and circle the best answer.

1. Lydia is calling . . .
   a. a friend.
   b. her teacher.
   c. her boss.

2. She will not be in the office . . .
   a. this afternoon.
   b. tomorrow.
   c. on Monday.

3. Who wants to play golf?
   a. Mrs. Tripplehorn.
   b. Mr. Aziz.
   c. Mr. Suzuki.

B Listen again and fill in Mr. Osborne's diary.

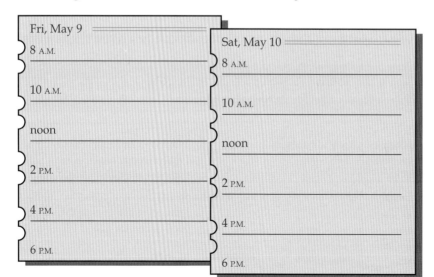

Fri, May 9
8 A.M.
10 A.M.
noon
2 P.M.
4 P.M.
6 P.M.

Sat, May 10
8 A.M.
10 A.M.
noon
2 P.M.
4 P.M.
6 P.M.

1. staff meeting
2. lunch with client
3. golf game
4. staff party
5. dentist's appointment

UNIT

How do you like to learn?

TASK
1

Student CD Track: **40**

A **Listen and circle the best response.**

1. a. Usually.
   b. Listening.
   c. Yes, I do.

2. a. Not very often.
   b. I try to guess.
   c. I prefer speaking.

3. a. Yes, I do, but I find it difficult.
   b. No, I prefer reading.
   c. I can't.

4. a. I like taking notes.
   b. Yes, they are.
   c. No, it makes me nervous.

5. a. Yes, I do.
   b. I'm not sure.
   c. I like learning languages.

6. a. Did you guess?
   b. Were you sure?
   c. Was it hard?

B **Listen again and check your answers.**

TASK
2

Student CD Track: **41**

A **Listen and circle the best answer.**

1. **Today is . . .**
   a. the first lesson of the semester.
   b. the last lesson of the semester.
   c. the first day of exams.

2. **According to the teacher, an active learner . . .**
   a. thinks about things very carefully.
   b. likes trying things out.
   c. enjoys individual problem-solving.

3. **The teacher suggests that . . .**
   a. active learners are better language learners.
   b. reflective learners are better language learners.
   c. one type of learner is not better than the other.

B **Listen again. Check (✔) your *own* answer (*a* or *b*) to each question you hear. Then check (✔) the kind of learner you are.**

1. _____ a. contribute a lot of my own ideas
   _____ b. listen to my classmates and then give my own opinion

2. _____ a. trying it out in conversation with other people
   _____ b. thinking carefully about it first, before trying it out

3. _____ a. with other people   _____ b. on my own

4. _____ a. when everybody brainstorms ideas together
   _____ b. when we all think about the issue individually, then compare our ideas

5. _____ a. role plays, pair work, and group work   _____ b. individual listening tasks

6. _____ a. I get bored quite easily.   _____ b. I find it quite easy to concentrate.

7. _____ a. outgoing   _____ b. thoughtful and reserved

_____ I am an active learner.   _____ I am a reflective learner.

Track	Content	
1	Announcement	
2	Unit 1	Task 1
3	Unit 1	Task 2
4	Unit 2	Task 1
5	Unit 2	Task 2
6	Unit 3	Task 1
7	Unit 3	Task 2
8	Unit 4	Task 1
9	Unit 4	Task 2
10	Unit 5	Task 1
11	Unit 5	Task 2
12	Unit 6	Task 1
13	Unit 6	Task 2
14	Unit 7	Task 1
15	Unit 7	Task 2
16	Unit 8	Task 1
17	Unit 8	Task 2
18	Unit 9	Task 1
19	Unit 9	Task 2
20	Unit 10	Task 1
21	Unit 10	Task 2

Track	Content	
22	Unit 11	Task 1
23	Unit 11	Task 2
24	Unit 12	Task 1
25	Unit 12	Task 2
26	Unit 13	Task 1
27	Unit 13	Task 2
28	Unit 14	Task 1
29	Unit 14	Task 2
30	Unit 15	Task 1
31	Unit 15	Task 2
32	Unit 16	Task 1
33	Unit 16	Task 2
34	Unit 17	Task 1
35	Unit 17	Task 2
36	Unit 18	Task 1
37	Unit 18	Task 2
38	Unit 19	Task 1
39	Unit 19	Task 2
40	Unit 20	Task 1
41	Unit 20	Task 2

See pages 108–127 for the Self Study Practice Tasks.